TRAINING
REALSCHULE

Josef Kilger

Englisch –
Comprehension 10. Klasse

Textaufgaben mit Lösungen

STARK

Umschlagbild: © Victor W. Fazio, III

ISBN: 3-89449-323-2

Inhalt

Autor: Josef Kilger

Vorwort

Liebe Schülerin, lieber Schüler,

dieses Buch hilft dir, dein Textverständnis zu verbessern, sodass du die Comprehension-Aufgaben des Englischunterrichts in der 10. Klasse gut bewältigen kannst. Die Grundlage hierfür bilden **zehn Übungstexte,** die abwechslungsreich gestaltet und spannend zu lesen sind. Jedem Text folgt ein **umfangreicher Übungsteil:**

- Mit den Fragen **zum Text** kannst du prüfen, ob du den Text auch wirklich verstanden hast. Die zustäzlichen Fragen ("additional" und "further questions") gehen über den Textinhalt hinaus und erweitern so deinen Wortschatz.
- Im Unterricht musst du viel übersetzen. Deshalb sind zehn **Übersetzungsaufgaben** angefügt. In diesen Sätzen ist viel Grammatik "versteckt", die du beim Übersetzen trainieren kannst.
- Mithilfe der **Grammatikaufgaben** kannst du gezielt einzelne grammatische Phänomene üben und Unsicherheiten beseitigen.
- Den **Lösungen** sind häufig ausführliche Hinweise angefügt, die dich auf die zugrundeliegende grammatische Regel der betreffenden Aufgabe aufmerksam machen. Wiederholungen sind hier beabsichtigt, damit du beim Üben sicherer wirst.
- Am Ende des Buches befindet sich eine **Liste mit grammatikalischen Ausdrücken** mit englischer Übersetzung, die dir beim Lösen der Grammatikaufgaben hilft.

Es empfiehlt sich, jeden Text gründlich durchzuarbeiten und alle Aufgaben dazu schriftlich zu lösen. Erst danach solltest du deine Lösungen mit denen im Buch vergleichen. Wenn du zusätzlich etwas für dein Hörverständnis tun möchtest, kannst du dir die Texte auch vorlesen lassen und dann die Aufgaben schriftlich lösen.
Zum Schluss möchte ich mich bei Erika Möckl bedanken, die als native speaker mein Manuskript durchgelesen hat.

Und nun viel Spaß und Erfolg beim Üben!

Josef Kilger

The Sparrow or How to Treat Animals

They spent their holidays in the Netherlands. When going home by car, they had to stop at a little town. They wanted to have lunch. Not finding a proper restaurant (some of them were extremely expensive, others overcrowded), they decided to go in a café. The waitress was young and neat, and Mr Joule was very pleased with her. His wife, however, didn't like it when her husband was continuously joking with the young girl. She was also against his ordering food which was no good for his health. I think it's time we inform you about Mr Joule. He was 70 years old, was suffering from heart attacks and of severe diabetes. His wife demanded that he had to order some salad and steamed rice. Mr Joule was a bit annoyed but he did what his wife wanted him to do. He drank a glass of mineral water. After paying the bill and leaving a tip on the table, they left the café. Mr Joule waved his hand secretly and the waitress smiled.

After having left the town, Mrs Joule drove extremely quickly. Her husband wasn't allowed to steer the car because of the reason mentioned above. He was sitting completely quietly watching the scenery. Being a fan of history and old buildings, he asked his wife to stop because he had seen an ancient tower on a hill. Hastily he got out of the car and hurried to the tower. Usually his wife didn't accompany him, as she didn't like this old stuff. Instead of watching old ruins, she preferred sitting in the car, reading thrilling detective stories. Mr Joule entered the tower nosily and went upstairs. Finally he got to the top storey. It was a round room with glass windows. There weren't any handles to open them. On the floor – and that is our surprise – a sparrow was sitting. When it saw our Mr Joule – don't forget his red face –, who was breathing heavily, it began to fly nervously against the window panes. But it couldn't escape. The noise of the bird's hitting against the panes was terrible and Mr Joule couldn't stand it. He wanted to catch the bird, running after him all the time. There were numerous situations when he could almost seize it, but the bird was quicker. Breathlessly, Mr Joule kept on running and after fifteen minutes he got hold of him. Their hearts were throbbing wildly, the sparrow's little heart and our Mr Joule's. He held the rescued bird between his hands and you could only see the little head and the blinking eyes of the exhausted bird.

Happily our "rescuer" carried the bird downstairs. His wife was coming to meet him at the entrance of the tower. After pressing the little fellow against his lips – it didn't like that – Mr Joule let it go and the bird flew away quickly into the air, chasing some insects.

Worksheet

I. Questions on the text

1. Answer each question on the text in a complete sentence.
   a) Why did our couple have their snack in a café?
   b) Why was Mr Joule happy when he saw the waitress and why wasn't Mrs Joule?
   c) Why wasn't Mr Joule permitted to eat everything he liked?
   d) Why do you think Mr Joule waved his hand secretly and why did the waitress smile?
   e) Why did Mrs Joule drive the car and not her husband? Think of the consequences or dangers.
   f) Why did Mrs Joule have to stop and why didn't she go with him?
   g) Why did our little sparrow fly around and against the window panes nervously?
   h) Why were both hearts throbbing, the little heart of our sparrow and Mr Joule's?
   i) Why was our rescuer happy (or what could have happened if Mr Joule hadn't caught the bird)?
   j) Why do you think his wife was coming to meet her husband?

2. Answer each additional question in a full sentence as well.
   a) Make a list of food you oughtn't to eat if you have had a heart attack (or a severe diabetes).
   b) What should you eat or drink instead?
   c) Do you think our Mr Joule is a sort of womanizer? I myself think he isn't.
   d) What's the job of a waiter or waitress and in which case do you leave a big tip?
   e) Why do you think Mrs Joule was driving extremely quickly?
   f) What was Mrs Joule's hobby?
   g) Why should she have accompanied Mr Joule? Think of what he was doing in the tower.

h) Why is it extraordinarily difficult to catch a sparrow, especially for our Mr Joule?

i) Why do you think Mr Joule "kissed" the bird?

j) How might the bird have got onto the top storey and not back?

3. Answer each further question in a full sentence.

a) Why is cruelty to animals truly detestable?

b) What can you as a young person, as a pupil, do in order to prevent that sort of cruelty?

c) The newspapers report on the transport of living animals to be slaughtered over long distances. What do you think of it?

d) Some people only eat food consisting of vegetables. Do you think that vegetarianism can solve the problem?

e) What do you think about experiments on animals?

f) Tell me something about the pros and cons of having a pet or pets.

g) Why should you call at the vet's when you've got a cat?

h) In some old people's homes they are allowed to have a pet. Why is it to be recommended?

i) In Great Britain there are strict quarantine rules for pets. What's the reason for that?

j) What do you know about the so-called "mad-cow-disease"?

II. Translation

Translate into German and mind the "hidden" grammar.

1. In welcher Jahreszeit sind die Vöglein dankbar, wenn du ein(e) besonders großzügige(r) Gastgeber(in) bist?

2. Mr Joule hatte Freude daran, seine "Gäste" im Garten zu beobachten.

3. Besonders im rauhen Winter bin ich zweifellos für sie verantwortlich.

4. Im letzten Sommer schaffte ich es, einen Sperling aufgrund meines Geschichtsinteresses zu befreien.

5. Ich gab nicht auf, den Sperling zu jagen, und es machte mir nichts aus, eine Zeit lang zu rennen.

6. Seit vielen Jahren bin ich überzeugt, dass man Tiere nicht einschließen soll (unser Sperling hatte sich aber, in der Tat, selber eingeschlossen).
7. Falls der Sperling einen Ausweg gehabt hätte, wäre er mir entkommen.
8. Abgesehen von zahlreichen Veröffentlichungen unterstütze ich den Tierschutz gelegentlich durch Vorträge.
9. Seit 1960 beeinflusst er die öffentliche Meinung.
10. Er gibt zu, dass er stolz darauf ist.

III. Grammar

1. Enter -ing or infinitive or both.
   a) Did he enjoy (see) ________________ old castles?
   b) She disliked (he / talk to) _________________ the young waitress.
   c) Mr Joule began (chase) _________________ the sparrow.
   d) Finally he managed (catch) ________________ it.
   e) He then decided (go) _________________ downstairs.

2. Enter the correct preposition and the correct forms.
   a) Mrs Joule insisted (her husband / order) _______________ steamed potatoes.
   b) She sometimes blamed him (flirt) ________________ with girls.
   c) Usually she prevents him (eat) _________________ cakes.
   d) Therefore Mr Joule must thank her (be) _______________ so strict.
   e) He can rely (she / help) _________________ him.

3. Complete the sentences either with the infinitive or preposition + -ing.
   a) Have we got time (have) _________________ lunch?
   b) There were many opportunities (visit) _______________ old towns.
   c) There is no reason (eat) _________________ a fatty sausage.
   d) You mustn't be in danger (get) _________________ a heart attack.
   e) Are you fond (chat) ________________ with the young waitresses?

4. Fill in the correct tense.
   a) Yesterday he (drink) ______________ two glasses of mineral water.
   b) Since 1980 they (make) _________________ many trips.
   c) For many years they (prefer) _____________________ to spend the holidays in the Netherlands.
   d) Their neighbours (travel) _____________ to the Bahamas next year.
   e) Mrs Joule (study) _________________ a leaflet now.

5. Translate, using the emphasizing pronoun.
   a) Mrs Joule fährt selber.
   b) Der Sperling konnte sich nicht selbst befreien.
   c) Mr Joule befreite ihn selber.
   d) Im Restaurant durfte Mr Joule nicht selber bestellen.
   e) "Ich kümmere mich (schon) selber um ihn."

6. The conditional clause: Fill in the correct forms.
   a) If you eat cakes you (become) ____________________ seriously ill.
   b) If the rescuer hadn't come, the bird (starve) ___________________.
   c) If Mr Joule (come) ________________ down earlier his wife would not have looked for him.
   d) I would get rather angry if you (eat) _________________ a steak.
   e) He must be sent to hospital if he (not / take) _______________ care of himself.

Uncle Charles or How to Educate Children

Things often aren't as they should be nor is the world perfect, neither the parents nor the children. If parents aren't a problem (sometimes) you needn't read this text. Do the exercises instead, then look up the solutions. But let us return to our Uncle Charles. Poor Charles, he never saw his dad, who was killed in the Second World War. His mum, a resolute person, had to educate little Charles all on her own. I don't believe that Uncle Charles – before he became my uncle – was difficult to educate but his mum did a lot of tricks to confuse little Charles, when he was nasty. She hid herself somewhere in the house, and Charles, who was totally afraid of being alone, searched the house, crying desperately. I completely agree with you that it was rather cruel and very hard to bear for an "abandoned" child. This was not the only trick which mum did. But I refuse to inform you as in the near future you will get married – the best and most ideal partner of course – and possibly you will have to educate children in a better way without doing tricks. But let's talk about Uncle Charles. When he was about 25 years old and the manager of a hotel, he often fell in love with blondes or brunettes, but there was his almighty mum: You are the manager of an exclusive hotel, you can't marry Caroline (a shop assistant), you can't marry Catherine (a nurse), you can't marry Cissy (a guide) etc. This was undoubtedly her best trick. Have you ever read of the Italian mamma who does everything for her son (a bachelor) and who is completely jealous when there is any young lady that wants to carry her "mammista" away. Uncle Charles lived with mamma in the same flat. They spent the holidays together in Italy many times but last year Charles met an extraordinarily beautiful lady who was a doctor at the hospital just in the same town where my uncle and mamma lived. It was a detour via Sirmione. Now mamma's trick was no longer effective as our lady doctor got much more salary than her "boy", who meanwhile was 32 years old. Mamma had to yield to things she couldn't change or influence any more.

When the wedding bells rang, she didn't look content and she even refused to eat anything at the wedding reception. Poor mamma! But when the young couple left for their honeymoon trip she kissed her son and even Diana, her daughter-in-law. "These things can't be changed", she sighed, went into the nearest café and ate two pieces of cream cake and drank two glasses of sherry. "Mamma mia", as the Italians say.

Worksheet

I. Questions on the text

1. Answer each question on the text in a complete sentence.
   a) Which sort of readers needn't read the text?
   b) Why did Charles not see his father, even as a baby (if a baby realises who he or she sees at all)? Give a detailed answer.
   c) What does the author of the text think of the educational tricks of Charles's mum? Enter typical phrases to back up your opinion.
   d) Why isn't the author of the text willing to inform you about other educational tricks or methods?
   e) Why was the almighty mum against Charles's marrying? Or was it simply a pretence (a wrong reason)?
   f) What's a typical Italian "mamma"?
   g) In which way was our Uncle Charles a genuine "mammista"?
   h) Why was mamma's trick no longer effective when her "boy" got to know a lady doctor?
   i) Why didn't she look content first and which situation shows that she yielded to the new facts?
   j) In which way did "mamma" console herself after the young couple had left for their honeymoon trip?

2. Answer each additional question in a full sentence as well.
   a) What is a resolute person?
   b) Do you think that dads are vital for the education or are women right who simply want to educate their children all by themselves?
   c) Do you remember a story of your childhood when you were totally desperate or sad?
   d) What other things are cruel, which things are unbearable to you?
   e) I wholly agree that you would educate your children better. Enter some characteristics.
   f) Could you imagine any professions of girls our mum would have accepted?

g) Why is a "permanent" bachelor the ideal son for a "mamma"?
h) When are you jealous? In some cases jealousy is a sort of addiction people can't escape from.
i) Why was it a detour or deviation in order to get to know each other in Italy?
j) Are there any things in your young life you must yield to (even reluctantly)?

3. Answer each further question in a sentence.
   a) Enter some items which demonstrate that the world isn't perfect. What can you do about that?
   b) I assume you are good at history. Tell me something about World War II.
   c) Give a short report of any wedding reception you've been to.
   d) What does the exclamation "Mamma mia" mean literally?
   e) Tell me where you would like to go on holiday and why you want to go there.
   f) Why do many people prefer going abroad to spending their holidays in Germany (Bavaria, on the North Sea shores, in the Luneburg Heath, the Black Forest ...)?
   g) Speak up in favour of one region mentioned in the brackets above.
   h) Do you know any differences between German or French or Italian restaurants?
   i) Why are holidays necessary?
   j) What do you think about holiday-makers whose main aim is to get to know new partners on their vacation?

II. Translation

Translate and mind the "hidden" grammar.

1. Kennst du viele "Mammas", die ihre Söhne nicht "forttragen" lassen wollen?
2. Angesichts der Tatsache, dass sie die Verbindung mit dem Sohn verlieren, wollen sie in der Regel die "Liebschaft" stoppen.

3. Sie konnte nicht umhin, das Mädchen, mit dem ihr Sohn tanzte, andauernd zu beobachten.
4. Nachdem sie absichtlich das Weinglas umgestürzt hatte, verließ sie wütend das Café.
5. Der Sohn musste aufhören zu tanzen und mit dem Kellner verhandeln.
6. Die junge Dame: "Du sollst unabhängig werden."
7. Sie bemerkte lächelnd: "Du solltest mich jetzt unterhalten."
8. Da er nicht nach seiner "Mamma" schaute und sich darauf verließ, dass sie wieder zurückkommen würde, hatte er Zeit, mit der jungen Dame zu reden.
9. "Mamma" hatte sich in der Garderobe aufgehalten, bevor sie zur Bushaltestelle ging.
10. Völlig unerwartet war sie nach Hause gefahren.

III. Grammar

1. Translate, using the verb + object + infinitive.
   a) Charles lud die Verkäuferin ein, mit ihm ins Kino zu gehen.
   b) Ihre Freundin ermutigte sie, die Einladung anzunehmen.
   c) Seit langem will er, dass sie ihn begleitet.
   d) "Kann ich mich darauf verlassen, dass du mitgehst, Caroline?"
   e) "Ich möchte gerne, dass sie im Kino nur Filme mit Humphrey Bogart zeigen."

2. Enter -ing or infinitive or both.
   a) He didn't manage (to be invited/being invited) ________________.
   b) She always hopes (to be collected/being collected) ____________.
   c) Do you mind (to be kissed/being kissed) ____________________?
   d) He continually denied (to meet her/meeting her) ______________ again.
   e) "I feel like (to buy/buying) __________________ flowers for her."

3. There are more ways of translating these sentences.
   a) Wer ist das Mädchen, mit dem du sprachst?
   b) Das Mädchen, mit dem er tanzte, heißt Cissy.
   c) Ich meine die Flitterwochen, die sie in Venedig verbrachten.
   d) Das Mädchen, das er immer einlädt, heißt Catherine.
   e) Das Hotel, in dem sie die Flitterwochen verbrachten, liegt am Meer.

4. Shorten the time clauses by -ing.
   a) After he had met her, he fell in love at once.
   b) After he has written the letter, he usually reads it twice.
   c) Before he posts it, he checks the address.
   d) As soon as he gets a letter from her, he is quite nervous.
   e) Before he opens the letter, he takes a deep happy breath.

5. Decide whether you must add an -ly or find a different phrase.
   a) He was dancing (happy) ____________________.
   b) The band played a (quick) ____________________ dance and he had to dance very (fast) ____________________.
   c) "Do you work (fast) _______________ when you get to know a girl?"
   d) "I think it's better to work (special, slow) ____________________. Girls don't like (fast) __________________ workers."
   e) "Speak (witty) _______________ and (friendly)__________________."

6. Put into indirect speech.
   a) Charles said: "I must dance with her."
   b) Charles said: "She mustn't go out."
   c) Charles said: "She has to be here."
   d) Charles said: "She may visit me today."
   e) Charles said: "She can cook well."

7. Translate into English.
   a) "Du solltest jetzt anrufen."
   b) Gestern sollte sie uns besuchen.
   c) Was soll ich tun?
   d) Du solltest doch heiraten, warum hast du nicht geheiratet?
   e) Er soll oft den Urlaub in Italien verbringen.

8. Shorten by using -ing.
   a) As "mamma" was against the marriage, they couldn't get married.
   b) Because I prefer blondes, I'm not interested in you.
   c) Because I have met Cissy, I don't want to see you any more.
   d) Because I was invited to the party, I didn't have time.
   e) Because she had been picked up by Charles, she couldn't help liking him.

How to Find Missing Members

Undoubtedly the town isn't very big. The old town itself is surrounded by strong walls with ditches and towers. Historically inclined people like this ancient town and you can see flocks of tourists every day, especially on Saturdays and Sundays. Critics say the town has recently developed into a modern industrial town with a lot of factories and offices and a lot of traffic is spoiling the romantic old city. Indeed, there are traffic jams. I simply can't agree with their views, as in the old town or city you don't notice the traffic as a wise council has established a lot of pedestrian zones and only a few one-way streets run across the city.

In order not to forget it, the city is round as if designed on a drawing board. The medieval city wall has therefore the shape of a circle and outside this one on the periphery or the outside edge so to speak there are five huge car parks for motor cars and of course for coaches. The council had the ditches simply filled up and got these precious spaces.

You might ask me why I am telling you these things. You'll see why below. The historical society – I am the chairman or president – went on a day excursion to that town. The excursionists were a mixed group of young people and people of every age but the majority were pensioners and other retired people. After departing, I took the microphone, welcomed everybody and told something about the town we excursionists intended to see. After arriving there, my main job was to help the bus driver to find the route to the car park at the swimming bath. Of course we were late and the guides had to wait almost half an hour for us. Before getting off the bus, I once again announced (microphone!) that everybody had to be back at four p.m. I haven't got the time to tell you anything about the sights we saw, the lunch in the restaurant etc. At four o'clock everybody was there, either sitting in the coach or standing outside and chatting. But stop for a short time, I must continue: Everyone was there but three members were missing. I don't want to tell you the names, I will simply call them missing person 1, 2 and 3. After half an hour person 1 came to the car park, totally exhausted, heavily sweating and with a red face. After drinking a mouthful of mineral water, he told us that he had been waiting at the wrong car park and, realising it was the wrong one, he went by bus – the merciful bus driver didn't even ask for the fare – for some distances. After one hour persons 2 and 3 were still missing. My club treasurer and I took a taxi and wanted to find them. Everybody was doubtful whether we would be lucky. The taxi driver was rather amused as we explained to him that we wanted to search the town. But after 15 minutes I saw the missing members walking very quickly out of a park. I shouted, "They are over there", the taxi driver braked immediately, we dragged and pushed them into the taxi, it looked like a kidnapping.

Worksheet

I. Questions on the text

1. Answer each question on the text in a complete sentence.
   a) Why are there so many tourists and visitors, especially at weekends?
   b) Some people think that the town is being spoilt. Can you tell me why?
   c) What does an industrial town look like?
   d) Why isn't the old town choked up with traffic and the air pollution isn't so high?
   e) Where are the car parks and how did the council get the particular spaces for them?
   f) Were the missing excursionists right to blame the chairman that they were lost? Give the reason(s) for your answer.
   g) Why did missing member number 1 arrive first? There is more than one reason.
   h) Why was the taxi driver amused?
   i) Why did the scene look like a kidnapping?
   j) Sum up: Why weren't all three members not able to get to the swimming baths in time?

2. Answer each additional question in a full sentence as well.
   a) Why is there a lot of traffic in an industrial town? Is the increase in traffic only due to industry?
   b) Why are there still people against pedestrian zones?
   c) Why do you think the author didn't tell you the names of the missing members?
   d) Why do you think everyone was doubtful whether the chairman and the treasurer would be able to find the two other missing members by taxi?
   e) Can you tell me any other reasons for taking a taxi?
   f) The job of a taxi driver is in some respects an interesting job. Can you tell me why?

g) In which way might the members of the club have "welcomed" the missing members?

h) One of the women was extremely nervous as one of the missing members was her husband who had been in hospital because of a heart attack. Could you tell me why?

i) What would you have said if you had been one of the missing members?

j) If you wanted to make fun of them, what could you say to them (provided you are in a good mood after waiting for almost one and a half hour)?

3. Answer each further question in a sentence.

a) Why aren't there town walls and ditches in modern towns any more (or why in the Middle Ages)?

b) What hobbies do historically inclined people enjoy?

c) What shouldn't you do in order to protect your environment?

d) Why is a one-way street better for the environment instead of streets with two or more lanes?

e) What's the purpose of a historical society or club?

f) There are also clubs for the conservation or protection of the environment. What are their aims?

g) What are the consequences of pollution?

h) Can you tell me anything about some environmentally friendly means of transport?

i) Let's go back to our excursion: Why do people go on an excursion?

j) What's the difference between a coach and a bus?

II. Translation

Translate and mind the "hidden" grammar.

1. Seit einem Jahr beabsichtigen die Mitglieder des Vereins, einen Ausflug zu machen.

2. Sie fahren gerne in alte Städte und es macht ihnen nichts aus, ganz lange Fahrten im Bus zu machen.

3. Viele könnten es sich sogar leisten, mehrere Tage in einer anderen Stadt zu verbringen, da sie schon Pensionisten sind.
4. Sie geben zu, geschichtsinteressiert zu sein und haben immer Lust, historische Städte zu besuchen.
5. Auch ich möchte gerne eine Fahrt machen, aber ich schaffe es gewöhnlich nicht, mich zu entscheiden, wohin.
6. Die Dame, mit der ich gerade rede, ist die Leiterin des Reisebüros (sie ist die charmanteste, die ich kenne.)
7. Die Zeitschrift, die ich seit einem Jahr lese, handelt von interessanten Reisen.
8. Das einzige Buch, an dem meine Freundin interessiert ist, ist das Kochbuch, aber sie ist die schlechteste Köchin auf der Welt.
9. Falls du meine Freundin triffst, frag sie nicht, warum der Taxifahrer immer heimlich im Restaurant isst.
10. Falls wieder zwei Ausflügler in mein Auto steigen, um ein verlorengegangenes Mitglied zu suchen, sage ich stolz, dass ich ein Fachmann darin bin.

III. Grammar

1. Fill in the correct tenses.
   a) Since 1980 they (go) ______________ on excursions.
   b) For five years they (visit) _____________ ancient towns in Bavaria.
   c) After they (depart) __________, the chairman took the microphone.
   d) "Wait a moment. I (announce) _______________ essential pieces of information after one minute."
   e) The weather forecast for the afternoon: The weather (be) _________ fine.

2. Enter -ing or infinitive or both.
   a) The chairman can't bear (speak) ___________ to chatting members.
   b) He continued (announce) __________ some important information.
   c) Everybody promised (come back) ________________ in time.
   d) They were all looking forward to (see) _____________ the Minster.
   e) In spite of (be) ______________ exhausted, even the older members took part in the long guided tour.

3. Shorten the clauses.
   a) Because they didn't find the way back, two members were rather nervous.
   b) As the chairman was rather angry, he didn't tell any jokes as he usually did.
   c) Before he told the driver to start, he counted his members.
   d) Do you remember the members who were lost in the town?
   e) In the ancient town there were many tourists who looked for/who were looking for a proper restaurant.

4. Write down different structures.
   a) The guide whom the tourists like best gets a prize from the mayor.
   b) The guide to whom the members listened is one of the best.
   c) Can you tell me the excursion to which everybody looks forward?
   d) Is that the trip for which the treasurer is responsible?
   e) The last trip was the best which they ever had.

5. Do the comparison.
   a) It was one of the (bad) ______________ trips.
   b) It was even (bad) _______________ than the trip this year.
   c) That trip was the (boring) ________________ trip.
   d) We hope the next trip will be (amusing) _______________ than the one this year.
   e) Organizing such a trip isn't the (simple) _______________ task.

6. The conditional clause: Fill in the correct forms.
   a) If they hadn't found them, the other members (be) _______________ rather nervous.
   b) "If I were you, I (not/look) _________for them as they are grown-ups."
   c) Don't enter if the guide (forbid) ________________ it.
   d) If you don't come back in time, everybody (get) _________________ annoyed.
   e) If such incidents happen once again, the next trips (cancel) _______.

7. -ly or not
   a) The chairman was (extreme) _______________ furious.
   b) The taxi driver drove (quick) ________________ than ever before.
   c) "Our" two members didn't look (happy) _____________ as they were tired.
   d) They felt rather (bad) ________________.
   e) They tried to defend themselves (fluent) ________________ but they did it (bad) _________________.

8. Indirect speech
   a) The chairman said: "Return in time."
   b) The chairman said: "Don't be late."
   c) The chairman said: "We will visit the fortress."
   d) The chairman said: "I have never seen this building."
   e) The chairman said: "We have to hurry now."

How to Get a Son-in-law

You might remember if you paid enough attention to your history teacher that in the Stone Age your great-grandfather (etc.), or one of your first ancestors did everything by himself. But in the course of time there has been some specialisation. Now in the last decade of the twentieth century there are many other specialists or different needs, even city companions for ladies and home-sitters for your house or flat when you go on holiday. The first is a new service indeed: The manageress of a firm is in a city and she wants to go out. Apart from being harassed or even attacked when going out or getting back to the hotel, it's much nicer to dine with someone. Of course, you must pay for it. It isn't free either to engage a homesitter. When our family – I didn't store the data in order to protect our private matters – left the town for the Caribbean Sea the homesitter was instructed thoroughly: 1. Watering the flowers 2. Feeding the dog and the cat 3. Getting the mail out of the mail box 4. Putting the dustbin can on the pavement for the refuse collection 5. Answering the telephone 6. Cleaning the room once a week – the family's cleaner, Mrs Porridger was supposed to help – and airing the rooms every day 7. Pulling down the blinds at night and pulling them up the next morning 8. Checking whether everything is in order etc.

You might accept the fact that our homesitter wasn't allowed to smoke or empty all the bottles of wine or cognac. No girl was permitted to stay during the night. But there was one exception. It was a rainy afternoon when the doorbell rang. Our homesitter went to the front door and there was a young brunette girl with a huge umbrella. She was rather beautiful as far as our homesitter could tell. She was wearing denim jeans and shoes with high heels and a green sweater. Our homesitter, a handsome young man as far as female acquaintances can tell, wasn't surprised, as the doorbell often rang and people delivered newspapers and magazines or wanted to sell various articles etc., but our pretty lady was totally amazed to see the young fellow there she had never seen before and who had opened the front door. She began to stutter nervously, "What are you doing here? Where are my parents?"

It was rather a funny situation when they were sitting together, having their dinner. But things can change or alter. It wasn't love at first sight – psychologists say it's no good and such a romance often ends abruptly –, but gradually they realized that the other person was nice and charming and they liked each other very much, in short, they fell in love.

When the family came back from their holiday, my wife, Mrs ... (no name, private matter) passed out when she saw her homesitter and her daughter holding hands.

Worksheet

I. Questions on the text

1. Answer each question on the text in a complete sentence.
   a) What is one difference between the Stone Age and one of the following ages?
   b) Why is the new service of a city companion necessary or a good idea?
   c) There was a long list of duties for the homesitter. Which ones are absolutely necessary so that a criminal person can't see that the house is vacant?
   d) What wasn't the homesitter allowed to do?
   e) Why wasn't our homesitter astonished that there was a young girl at the front door?
   f) Why did the young girl stutter then?
   g) Why was it a funny situation when they had dinner?
   h) It wasn't love at first sight, but how was it then that they fell in love?
   i) Why did Mrs X pass out when she saw the homesitter with her daughter?
   j) The story ends up abruptly. Which passage in the text shows you that the romance continued?

2. Answer each additional question in a full sentence as well.
   a) What is an ancestor?
   b) What is the difference between a house and a flat?
   c) Why must the rooms be cleaned and aired?
   d) Why must you water the plants?
   e) What else might be checked on?
   f) Why do you think smoking was forbidden and drinking alcohol as well?
   g) When are you so amazed that you begin to stutter?
   h) Which passage of the text shows you that the author is male or female?

i) Why do you think psychologists warn about love at first sight?

j) But why is love at first sight rather usual?

3. Answer each further question in a sentence.

   a) Which other ages or periods can you name? Enter a characteristic feature of each age.

   b) Why is specialisation increasing even more?

   c) Why are there more and more firms which offer home sitting or protecting houses or factories and even people?

   d) Which qualities must a homesitter have and why is his employer concerned that he doesn't break the rules or that there isn't any black sheep among them?

   e) What is a black sheep in a family? Where does the term come from?

   f) The text tells us a rather unusual way of getting to know each other. Can you tell me other ways of getting to know a girl/young man?

   g) Are there any tricks or effective ways of starting a conversation with a person of the other sex?

   h) In which way did our parents or grandparents get to know each other? Is it really simpler for the younger generation to get to know people?

   i) Let's talk once again about a city companion. Which qualities must he have?

   j) In a leaflet I found the notice that the job of a city companion ends at the hotel entrance or in the hotel bar. Is it a good regulation?

II. Translation

Translate into English and mind the "hidden" grammar.

1. Es gab bis jetzt nicht nur Spezialisierung und diesen oder jenen neuen Dienst, auch die Gesellschaft veränderte sich.

2. Die Welt ist kleiner geworden, es gibt große Minderheiten. Viele verlassen ihr Heimatland und wandern ein, in der Hoffnung, ein besseres und freieres Leben führen zu können.

3. Die Grundrechte wie z. B. Redefreiheit, Versammlungsfreiheit, Religionsfreiheit usw. werden nicht überall auf der Welt geachtet.

4. Die gesellschaftlichen Probleme werden noch gesteigert durch die hohe Arbeitslosigkeit, besonders auch der Jugendarbeitslosigkeit. Viele haben auch Schwierigkeiten, eine Wohnung zu finden.
5. Auch in Deutschland werden die Obdachlosen immer mehr.
6. Wegen der steigenden Kriminalitätsrate sind viele gezwungen, während des Urlaubs das Haus bewachen zu lassen oder einen sogenannten Hausaufpasser zu engagieren.
7. Der Grund, dass Frauen mit einem Stadtbegleiter ausgehen, ist in der Großstadt verständlich.
8. "Ich will, dass Sie mich begleiten. Falls Sie keine Zeit haben, bleibe ich im Hotel."
9. "Nur wenn meine Dame nicht käme, würde ich mit Ihnen zum Italiener gehen."
10. "Wenn Sie mich eher angerufen hätten, hätte ich Sie gerne ausgeführt. Es wäre ein Vergnügen gewesen."

III. Grammar

1. Fill in the correct tenses.
   a) Many years ago I (not / pay) _______________ any attention to my history teacher.
   b) Since 1985 he (deal) ___________________ with his ancestors.
   c) For many years he (work) ___________ with a house sitting service.
   d) While he (sit) ______________ in the living-room, the doorbell rang.
   e) By the year 2010, he (earn) ________ enough money to quit the job.

2. Translate and decide whether infinitive or -ing.
   a) "Ich erwarte, dass Sie die Blumen gießen."
   b) "Kann ich damit rechnen, dass Sie Hund und Katze füttern?"
   c) "Ich will nicht, dass der Hausaufpasser raucht."
   d) "Es war nicht taktvoll, dass er sich in meiner Abwesenheit mit der Tochter befreundete."
   e) "Aber es war wichtig für uns, einen Aufpasser zu haben."

3. Translate and decide whether -ing or infinitive or both.
   a) Ich bin dagegen, dass er sie heiratet.
   b) Natürlich kann er sich nicht (dafür) entschuldigen, dass er sich verliebt hat.
   c) Ich denke nicht daran, meine Verwandten zu informieren.
   d) Ich bin es gewohnt, dass sie mir auch nichts erzählen.
   e) Aber ich könnte stolz sein, einen so gutaussehenden Schwiegersohn zu bekommen.

4. Do the comparison.
   a) The city companion was (clever) ____________ than anybody else.
   b) "The more wine you drink the (good) _____________ for me as you must pay for each hour."
   c) "The less money the (few) ___________ your friends", some people say.
   d) "I (little) ______________ expected that you would criticise me."
   e) Don't ask (far) ______________ questions.

5. Change from active to passive. In some cases you can leave out the by-agent.
   a) Our ancestors made almost everything all by themselves.
   b) Unfortunately, guys sometimes harass ladies.
   c) Can the companion protect her?
   d) Since 1990 I have accompanied single ladies.
   e) You should hire a companion.

6. This translation tests your knowledge on the German term "lassen".
   a) Sie ließ ihn fünfmal anrufen; aber er wollte das nicht.
   b) Er ließ die Dame warten.
   c) Sie ließ ihre Handtasche im Restaurant zurück.
   d) Bitte lassen Sie mich Fragen stellen.
   e) "Wo lassen Sie ihre Haare schneiden?"

7. Write down the reported questions.
   a) The companion continued asking: "Where do you live?"
   b) The companion continued asking: "Must you work hard?"
   c) The companion continued asking: "How long have you been married?"
   d) The companion continued asking: "Do you like modern music?"
   e) The companion continued asking: "Did you attend the concert yesterday?"

8. The conditional clause: Fill in the correct forms.
   a) If the homesitter hadn't gone to the door he (not/meet) ___________ the girl.
   b) You (may) _____________ stay if you are the homesitter.
   c) If he didn't get enough money he (might) _____________ complain.
   d) If he hadn't been the homesitter he (could not get) _____________ to know the girl.
   e) If he hadn't done his job well he (must) _____________ give some money back.

The Tax Office

Everybody knows that there are jobs or occupations or professions where you don't need a big office or a lot of employees to get a lot of money. I am not thinking of any stars, film stars, tennis stars, etc. I am merely thinking of an estate agent. It's a business for ladies and gentlemen, and even the toughest emancipationists can't complain. The only thing you must have is a computer and telephone and be clever and alert enough to get to know a lot of people. Our agent was a widow and the only hobby she had was going hunting. For that purpose she had a hunting dog called Houndy. He was a clever and well-trained hound and ready to obey his mistress. When our agent drove into the garage, Houndy began to bark enthusiastically.

May I remind you of the story everybody talked about? I hope you remember it. When our lady was at a hunters' meeting some criminals, nobody knows how many, entered the house but Houndy the guardian started barking frantically. I have heard of gangsters who kill people in cold blood but they can't do any harm to an animal. Houndy could look so true-heartedly. I don't know whether the gangsters knew about Houndy but one of them produced a sausage out of his pocket. While Houndy was eating the "present", another burglar held the dog and a third gangster gave him a narcotic injection with a syringe. After a short while our Houndy commenced to "sleep" on the carpet.

When our estate agent came home, she discovered Houndy, who was still a bit confused and he didn't even welcome his mistress by barking. Our agent also noticed that the safe had been opened by force or rather with chisels and a hammer. The only things she found in it were some envelopes and forms.

You could read in the "Echo" that approximately GBP 100,000 had been stolen. Being a clever person – see above, a special qualification for that occupation, indeed –, the agent had taken out an insurance policy against theft, burglary and robbery.

Some experts found out by examining the safe that it had been locked before the gangsters came. The insurance company had to pay the sum reluctantly though. But don't forget the tax office. In her tax return our agent only declared a yearly income of some GBP 25,000. Why was it then that the tax inspectors wondered that so much money was kept in the safe? "A tremendously high percentage of my money went into tax", our lady complained. "And the fine for a tax-dodger isn't low, indeed", she grumbled.

Worksheet

I. Questions on the text

1. Answer each question on the text in a complete sentence.
   a) Why can't even the toughest emancipationist be envious of the job of an estate agent?
   b) Why did our agent own a hound? Don't simply copy the text.
   c) Our agent liked her dog as it had two good qualities. Tell me what they were.
   d) The author has heard of gangsters who couldn't do any harm to animals. One quality of Houndy might have persuaded the gang additionally not to do any harm to him.
   e) Why was the sausage no real present of an animal-lover in general and especially not of a dog lover?
   f) When going into the garage our agent was astonished. What was she astonished at?
   g) Why did the gangsters have to open the safe by force (a simple question indeed)?
   h) Why was our agent a clever person?
   i) Why did the insurance company have to pay the full sum in the end?
   j) Why couldn't our agent reserve that money for herself (or the full sum of it)?

2. Answer each additional question in a full sentence as well.
   a) What is the job of an estate agent? Do you know any other agents that work in agencies of course?
   b) Why must an agent be clever and alert enough and why is it practical and convenient to know a lot of people?
   c) Where else do you have narcotic injections and why?
   d) What does a door or a window or a car look like when somebody has tried to open it by force and unfortunately succeeded?
   e) What can people insure themselves against? I think there are a lot of insurances.

f) Do you think it was robbery not only burglary as the dog was a sort of victim?

g) In this case the term victim is necessary. Define generally what a victim is.

h) Why should you lock your house, car etc.?

i) What is a tax return?

j) Apart from the taxes due, our agent had to pay an additional sum of money. Can you tell me why?

3. Answer each further question in a sentence.

a) What's the difference between job, occupation and profession?

b) Having answered the first question you may be able to tell me in which jobs (professions, occupations) you need bigger offices or a lot of employees.

c) What is an emancipationist?

d) What is a widow, which problems is she often concerned with, what does she live on usually?

e) Make a list of crimes.

f) Which things should you store in a safe?

g) There are different sorts of taxes. Write down some of them.

h) Why do some tax-payers ask a tax expert or tax consultant to help them?

i) What are direct or indirect taxes?

j) Why are taxes absolutely necessary (unfortunately)?

II. Translation

Translate and mind the "hidden" grammar.

1. Der Immobilienmakler muss nicht ein langes Studium abschließen, er braucht nur einen Computer und ein Telefon.

2. Natürlich muss er ein äußerst gutes Benehmen haben und es muss ihm gelingen, viel zu verkaufen.

3. Bevor Sie daran denken, das Haus zu verkaufen, lassen Sie ein Inserat in die Zeitung setzen. Das ist billiger als die Gebühren für den Makler.

4. Sicherlich müssen Sie viel Zeit verbringen, den möglichen Käufern das Haus, das Sie verkaufen wollen, zu zeigen.
5. Sobald Sie sehen, dass jemand interessiert ist, sollten Sie einen Vertrag aufsetzen (übrigens gibt es auch ein Formblatt).
6. Sie können den Mann aber nicht hindern, dass er geht, Sie können auch nicht zu einem Gericht gehen, einen Anwalt bitten. Auch das oberste Gericht kann nicht helfen.
7. Sie brauchen aber Hilfe durch einen Anwalt, falls der Steuerprüfer kommt und alle Rechnungen überprüft.
8. Die Steuer muss gezahlt werden, auch wenn Sie dagegen sind und es satt haben, zu zahlen. Niemand mag gerne Steuern zahlen.
9. Der Staat besteht darauf, dass wir das tun, und Sie können sich nicht entschuldigen, dass Sie es vergessen haben.
10. Sie können das Problem nicht einfach dadurch lösen, indem Sie in ein Steuerparadies auswandern, abgesehen davon, dass Ihre Ehefrau dagegen ist.

III. Grammar

1. Here are some answers. Ask the questions.
   a) "Yes, I must lock the safe."
   b) "No, you needn't buy a better safe."
   c) "Yes, I had to take out an insurance policy."
   d) "No, you mustn't dodge the tax."
   e) "Yes, I was at the meeting."

2. Decide whether -ly or not.
   a) Did the gangsters search the house (systematic)________________?
   b) The dog barked (enthusiastic) ___________________.
   c) The dog was (simple) __________________ true-hearted.

d) He looked (complete / true-hearted) ___________________.

e) The sausage tasted (extraordinary / good) ____________________.

3. Write down -ing or infinitive. Add the preposition if necessary.

a) There are a lot of ways (open) ________________ a safe.

b) "Have you got an opportunity (go) ______________ hunting?"

c) "I have no time (hunt) _______________."

d) "Have you got any difficulty (chase) __________________ a wild animal?"

e) Many came in the hope (kill) ______________ many animals.

4. Shorten the clauses.

a) After the dog has heard its master, it begins to bark.

b) After she had left the house, she went to a hunters' assembly.

c) Before she entered the house, she shouted "Houndy!"

d) There was a tax inspector who checked/was checking the receipts.

e) Because she didn't fill in the forms correctly, she was fined.

5. Translate into English.

a) Sie hat den Safe reparieren lassen.

b) Der Einbruch war ihr schlimmstes Erlebnis.

c) "Was soll ich tun?"

d) "Ich sollte jetzt die Versicherung anrufen."

e) "Ich konnte nicht eher heimkommen."

6. Conditional clause: Enter the correct forms.

a) If the tax inspector (not / read) _________________ about it in the newspaper, he wouldn't have come.

b) "If the dose isn't strong enough, we (must) _______________ give Houndy a second injection."

c) "If I were you, I (not / do) _________________ that."

d) "If I (hear) ________________ a noise, I would run away."

e) If Houndy hadn't been so true-hearted, the gangsters (not / be) ___________ "successful".

7. Once again: Decide whether -ing or not or both, occasionally you must fill in a preposition.
   a) The widow was keen (get) ________________ a lot of money.
   b) She wasn't afraid (live) __________________ alone in the house.
   c) She was rather interested (chairman / kill)__________ wild animals.
   d) "But I am tired (you / ask) _______________ me questions."
   e) Apart (have)_____________ a lot of money, she was a charming lady indeed.

How to Find Time for Thinking

An experienced artillerist knows that you have to hold your hands over your ears so that the bang of the gun can't destroy the tympanic membrane in your ears. Even the recruits learn that in their first instructions. If you are a rooky (a new soldier) in the armed forces you will have to learn a lot of things. First of all you have to obey the sergeants or other military people of a higher rank. Wait a moment: I am a pupil and not a rooky and I am forced to do what other people (teachers) want me to do. I've never heard that there are barracks. Of course there aren't but discipline is undoubtedly necessary for thinking and learning. If there is a tremendous noise and total chaos in the classroom no one can listen to the teacher's explanations. Last Monday there was a funny situation: Our maths teacher Mr Ritemayor – he likes to repeat things as a pedagogical trick – said that a lot of scientists and mathematicians and geometricians have tried in vain to transform a circle into a square by a more or less simple construction. A lot of maths teachers still dream of the so-called quadrature of the circle, I am convinced Mr Ritemayor himself does. Only five minutes before the schoolbell rang, my neighbour put up his hand and asked our Mr Ritemayor whether he knew any mathematician who had succeeded in constructing a square out of a circle. I needn't inform you about the teacher's reaction ...

Let us make an attempt to understand my neighbour's stupid and superfluous question. The first attempt: My neighbour intended to put the teacher's back up. Comment: No, he is a completely polite fellow. The second attempt: My neighbour wasn't dreaming of the quadrature of the circle, he was dreaming of his football team – top league? – or of some blonde. Comment: Might be. The third attempt: He simply didn't hear what the maths teacher was teaching. He (and I do occasionally, too) gets lots of pieces of information daily: The radio and the TV pour thousands of items over us, sounds and pictures in addition the computer and the internet with their virtual world. And we can't escape and put up an umbrella like a shelter against it all. Some of our contemporaries are even addicts who can't free themselves from watching TV or listening to the radio continuously. Our teachers at school are at a disadvantage compared with the radio or screen stars. The teachers and parents often complain about the lack of the pupils' attention. "You must learn to listen to the teachers or the foreman or the general. Fatal accidents might happen if you don't pay attention to the commander's orders. As I want to be a nurse I had my interview last Friday. The doctor wasn't only interested in my marks, he also did a psychological check-up, which took the full afternoon, in order to see whether I was able to listen or to concentrate. I learnt after the test what the check-up was for.

Worksheet

I. Questions on the text

1. Answer each question on the text in a complete sentence.
   a) In which part of the army can your tympanic membranes be injured and why?
   b) Why do the recruits learn about it in their very first lessons?
   c) What do a recruit and a pupil have in common?
   d) Why is discipline necessary at school?
   e) Why did my neighbour ask Mr Ritemayor whether there was a mathematician who had been able to solve the quadrature of the circle?
   f) Why is it becoming more and more difficult to listen to something attentively or carefully?
   g) What is a TV or internet addict?
   h) Say in your own words why teachers are at a disadvantage.
   i) When it is very dangerous or unfortunate if you don't listen carefully? Can you tell me why?
   j) What was the doctor interested in?

2. Answer each additional question in a full sentence as well.
   a) Where else do people hold their hands over their ears?
   b) Why is repeating things a good pedagogical trick?
   c) Which things must you use to transform any geometrical figure by construction?
   d) What is the quadrature of the circle?
   e) What would happen if Mr Ritemayor found out the way of transforming a circle into a square?
   f) What was the teacher's reaction like after my neighbour's question?
   g) What's a superfluous question? Ask me any question of that kind.
   h) Where does the term shelter come from and what is it?
   i) Why do you think a nurse must be thoroughly attentive?
   j) Why wasn't the girl told what the check-up was for?

3. Answer each further question in a sentence.
   a) What is a recruit or rooky?
   b) Write down some ranks in the army or navy or air force.
   c) Why are there barracks?
   d) Can you tell me any other funny situation?
   e) What is a completely polite fellow?
   f) Think up a commercial (an advertising spot).
   g) What is a virtual world or virtual reality?
   h) In which ways can we help addicts?
   i) What do pupils usually do before an interview?
   j) Write down five questions the personnel manager might ask you.

II. Translation

Translate into English and mind the "hidden" grammar.

1. Du musst zugeben, dass der General erfahrener ist als der Rekrut, und deshalb musst du ihm gehorchen.
2. Wenn ein Rekrut weniger Geld hat, muss er nicht notwendigerweise weniger Freunde (oder Freundinnen) haben.
3. Je höher der Rang, desto weniger Freunde hat jemand oder nur solche, die sich Vorteile erwarten.
4. Disziplin in der Armee ist genauso notwendig wie in der Schule, oder glaubst du eventuell, in der Schule ist sie nicht so wichtig?
5. Leider glauben viele Schüler, besonders Mädchen: "Je jünger ein Lehrer, desto besser, je älter, desto schlechter". Oder sind die älteren menschlicher und verständnisvoller? Hat noch jemand weitere Fragen?
6. Sogar der Schönste, der Jüngste, der Eleganteste, der Charmanteste will, dass man etwas lernt und Fähigkeiten erlangt.
7. Wollen Schüler, dass sich der Lehrer nach der neuesten Mode kleidet? Ist das wesentlich? Eine anonyme Umfrage in der Klasse zeigte, dass eine Krawatte allgemein abgelehnt wird.

8. Sandra, mit der ich immer Tennis spiele, hasst Krawatten und Anzüge, sie glaubt, nur Jeans, die aus den Staaten eingeführt werden, sind modisch.
9. Monica, deren Vater einen Modeladen hat, mag nur Anzüge, die in Italien hergestellt werden.
10. Kennst du die zwei Blondinen im Jeansladen, Cissy und Mary, von denen eine selber Schneiderin ist? Ich kenne ein Mädchen, das elegante Seidenblusen und schwarze Röcke trägt.

III. Grammar

1. Put into reported speech.
   a) The teacher said/had said/would say: "Pay attention."
   b) The teacher said: "In my lessons there is no chaos."
   c) The teacher said: "We must draw a circle now."
   d) The teacher said: "I can't solve the problem of the quadrature of the circle."
   e) The teacher said: "We should give up."

2. The comparison: Enter the correct forms.
   a) Mr Ritemayor is the (skilful) _______________ teacher.
   b) There isn't the (little) _______________ noise in the classroom.
   c) He works (quick) _________________ than other teachers, even (fast) ______________ than Mr Heetsy.
   d) The (much) ________ he demands the (good) _________ the pupils.
   e) The pupils are the (good) ______________ in spite of getting (little) ___________ homework and (few) ___________ tests than last year.

3. Translate into English and mind the "hidden" grammar.
   a) Die Quadratur des Kreises ist genau so schwierig wie das Herstellen von Benzin aus Wasser.
   b) Der Mathematiklehrer trägt die neuesten Anzüge.
   c) Er wohnt weit weg, aber nicht so weit wie Mr Heetsy, der eine weitere Strecke fahren muss.

d) Gestern traf ich einen Lehrer, der jeden Tag 2 ½ Stunden mit dem Zug fährt.
e) Er lebt in einem Haus, das im späten 19. Jahrhundert gebaut wurde.
f) Die Informationen werden nicht mehr wahrgenommen.
g) Im Computer wird die wirkliche Welt nachgeahmt.
h) Seit Jahrzehnten beschäftigen sich Wissenschaftler mit dem "Rechner".
i) Seit geraumer Zeit wird der Computer auch im Unterricht eingesetzt.
j) Optimisten sagen voraus, dass bis zum Jahr 2000 in jedem Haushalt ein Computer verwendet (werden) wird.

4. Ask questions.
   a) Yes, he likes maths.
   b) No, he needn't attend special courses.
   c) No, he mustn't give up his plans.
   d) Yes, for many years he has studied the problem.
   e) Yes, he will succeed.

How to Become More Interesting

"I won't allow you to go out in this mini skirt". Or: "We don't expect you to wear these tight black jeans and those shoes with the high heels". A lot of you youngsters have often heard these remarks and the result was either that you stayed at home reluctantly and lay sulkily on the couch in your room, the doors locked of course, or the result was that you rushed out of the house and did it for spite. Your friends may have encouraged and persuaded you to telephone your parents: "I know, you expect me to put on things you think are fashionable for a young girl but I prefer to wear things which I think suit me. You can count on me learning at school etc. ..." If your parents are sensible people their conversation might be like this. Dad: "I believe that our daughter is no longer a child, she has taken the first step towards becoming grown-up." Mum: "She is still our daughter, we are a respected family and I dislike her walking in the street in these clothes. I really mind her wearing tight jeans. There are such friendly neighbours who don't hesitate to stick their noses into our business or turn their noses up at our daughter."

There are many other things youngsters can be blamed for. You can dye your hair preferably green, or green and red, you can wear old-fashioned trousers or blouses you found in the attic, you can put on intentionally torn jeans with black lacy underwear everybody can see through. You can have your ear pierced – not shocking at all as even granny had it done –, you can have your nose or eye-lid pierced or even your skin to decorate your navel with a ring. I heard of a young girl who wanted to pierce all by herself but passed out immediately and was discovered unconscious by her mum.

Piercing is necessary to wear rings in your eye-lid, nose, lips. Your dad can't help saying that only bulls have got such a nose-ring. I don't know many young people who wear rings in that way, it's a fashion which won't be in for very long. Even the strictest parents can't prevent their children from doing something which seems "modern", even the most diplomatic parents don't often find any way of stopping new habits.

When you plan to be a grown-up don't keep away from arguments but try to find some solutions. Parents can be a problem, can't they?

Worksheet

I. Questions on the text

1. Answer each question on the text in a complete sentence.
   a) In which two ways can young people react when something isn't allowed? Don't copy the text, answer as briefly as you can.
   b) Why do many girls like to wear these or those things?
   c) Who is more understanding (at least in our text), dad or mum? Write down a short reason for your answer.
   d) The text says that many things have been done before. Write down the items.
   e) Which new fashion is shocking even for sympathetic parents?
   f) Why was the young girl found unconscious?
   g) What do people usually say when they see youngsters with nose-rings (not only dads with nerve-racking children)?
   h) Can parents hope that things will change some time?
   i) Can parents be blamed for their children's habits?
   j) You shouldn't knock your head against the wall when young. What should you do instead, according to the text?

2. Answer each additional question in a full sentence as well.
   a) What else can you do to become more interesting or to draw attention to yourself?
   b) The text begins with two typical remarks of parents. Write down other "bans".
   c) When did you lie sulkily on your couch last time?
   d) Tell me something about your mood or feelings when you did something for spite.
   e) Why are arguments necessary for the development of a young person?
   f) Stick your nose into another person's business. Write down two items in direct speech (with quotation marks).
   g) When do you turn your nose up at people?

h) Why must a bull have a nose-ring?

i) Can you tell me something about other fashionable things in the last decade of the twentieth century?

j) Despite of all the conflicts parents are vital for you. Write down two or three items.

3. Answer each further question in a sentence.

a) Do you think that the image of young people is influenced or formed by the media?

b) In which way can young people depend on the commercials (and grown-ups as well)?

c) Which sort of people are heroes for young people?

d) Do you agree that "fine feathers make fine birds"?

e) Can you tell me any situations in which special clothing is appropriate and even "progressive" youngsters can't ignore it?

f) What's your opinion about sexy clothes in your case or generally?

g) In which period of the year are you allowed to dress up and why do people do so?

h) Either you buy a suit or costume off the peg or you have it made by a tailor(ess). Discuss the pros and cons.

i) What's formal and casual clothing or wear?

j) Why is the fashion industry interested in frequent changes and why are younger people the better customers?

II. Translation

Translate and mind the "hidden" grammar.

1. Bevor das Mädchen sich verärgert auf die Couch legte, schloss sie die Tür ab.

2. Während sie eine Zeitschrift, die sie erst am Tag zuvor gekauft hatte, las, hörte sie (gleichzeitig) Radio.

3. Nachdem sie einen außerordentlich interessanten Artikel gelesen hatte und sich beruhigt hatte, diskutierte sie darüber mit ihrer Mutter.

4. Gewöhnlich wird sie ruhiger, nachdem sie etwas Interessantes gelesen hat.
5. Die alten Seidenblusen, die sie auf dem Speicher fand, gehörten einst ihrer Tante.
6. Die Freundin, die zerrissene Jeans trägt, hat meiner Ansicht nach die strengsten Eltern, aber sie können sie nicht abhalten, diese Jeans zu tragen.
7. Die Jeans, die im Supermarkt verkauft werden, sind nicht so schick wie die aus der Modeboutique, nicht wahr?
8. Nachdem ihr gesagt wurde, neue Kleider zu kaufen, fuhr sie mit ihrer Freundin nach München.
9. Nachdem sie eingekauft hatten, gingen sie in die Eisdiele und bestellten Eis.
10. Nachdem sie heimgekommen waren, tranken sie noch Kaffee, bevor sie die Kleidung auspackten.

III. Grammar

1. Change the -ing-clause into a clause with a conjunction or pronoun.
   a) Not liking ordinary trousers, she wore tight black jeans.
   b) The person over there, wearing high heels, is her cousin.
   c) After lying on the couch, she went shopping.
   d) Before trying the things on, she was in 20 shops at least.
   e) Not liking mini skirts, her mum always starts arguing about them.

2. Change into -ing-clauses.
   a) Because I was shouted at wearing these jeans, I was lying sulkily on the couch.
   b) As she saw my pierced navel, she was shocked.
   c) The blouses which were bought in Paris are over there.
   d) After she had her lips pierced, she went to the café.
   e) Before the jeans are sold, they are displayed in the shop window.

3. Translate into English.
   a) Sie ließ sich die Ohren durchstechen.
   b) Ich bin dagegen, dass du diese schwarze Unterwäsche trägst.
   c) Du solltest die Jeans nicht absichtlich zerreißen.
   d) Du irrst dich, wenn du meinst, das ist super.
   e) Ich frage mich, warum du dich weigerst, es zu tun. Du belastest dich (selber).

4. Translate.
   a) Wir sind (es) alle gewohnt, diese Kleidung zu tragen.
   b) Diese Jeans ist gut in der Freizeit zu tragen.
   c) Ohne sie zu probieren solltest du sie nicht kaufen.
   d) Anstatt zu jammern solltest du andere aussuchen.
   e) Ich habe Freude daran, viele Jeans zu haben.

5. Write down relative clauses.
   a) Do you know the girl ___________ parents are jeans manufacturers?
   b) Cissy Cranford ______________ is 22 years old, is a friend of mine.
   c) This jewel ring ____________ cost GBP 5,000 belongs to my mum.
   d) The girl ________________ I went shopping hates piercing.
   e) Superstar is the most elegant shop ______________ you can find in the town.

6. Enter "Nicht wahr" or "oder?".
   a) Worn jeans aren't chic, __________________?
   b) A formal dress can be super, __________________?
   c) We expect a big choice, __________________?
   d) We will find something, __________________?
   e) We won't be disappointed, __________________?

The Grand Ball

There was a longer stop at the railway station before he could change. A sign said: The last train 11.20 p.m. He noticed a colourful poster: Grand Ball of the fire brigade today. There were two dancers who were dancing under or between long blue, yellow and red paper streamers. The gentleman was wearing a fire brigade uniform and a brass helmet, the lady a black body suit and black stockings with garters. After having glanced at the poster for a long time, he decided to attend the ball. The admission was free. The fire brigade band played a mixture of old music and modern hits. The ballroom was full of nice and exciting girls. As he wasn't a quick worker he sat at a table, watching the dancers and the girls, and drank or rather sipped his drink. Then he saw her: Long legs, a green strapless ball dress, fair hair, altogether simply fascinating.

They danced enthusiastically, they devoted themselves totally to dancing, they laughed, they were both in extremely high spirits. He looked deeply into her blue eyes, he touched her silky hair by chance, they even kissed enthusiastically and gently and tenderly.

Secretly he glanced at his wristwatch and noticed that it was 10.45 p.m. He said he had to catch the train. When the band ceased playing they went back to her table. Hastily he asked her for her address, she gave him a little note with the address on it. She seemed to be a bit sad or angry.

Next morning he wrote a letter full of compliments, swearing his true love and asking for a date. He posted the letter without the sender. Think of nosy parents.

Every day he waited for the postman, he opened the mailbox full of hope, no letter there ... After some weeks his dad wanted to speak to him in private. His dad wasn't angry, he was even somewhat amused. He produced a letter out of his pocket, crumpled, and waved it in front of our letter-writer's eyes. Blushing, he recognized his letter, his envelope, a lot of postmarks and adhesive labels on it. As there was no sender on the envelope a special team of the GPO had opened it to find out the sender. The girl's address was not hers at all, the girl had made the whole thing up. Who can understand women or girls?

Worksheet

I. Questions on the text

1. Answer each question on the text in a complete sentence.
   a) Why did the young passenger glance at the poster?
   b) Why was he able to attend the fire brigade ball?
   c) Tell me in your own words why he sat and watched the dancers first?
   d) Which passage in the text shows that they liked each other?
   e) Why did he secretly glance at his wristwatch?
   f) How would the girl have reacted if she had seen it?
   g) Why do you think she was a bit sad or angry?
   h) Why didn't our young dancer write the sender on the envelope?
   i) Why was dad a bit amused and why did the boy blush?
   j) Think of the fire brigade ball. Why did the girl give him an "invented" address?

2. Answer each additional question in a full sentence as well.
   a) When must a passenger change?
   b) As the admission was free, in which way do you think the fire brigade got some money for the costs?
   c) Why do you think the band played old and modern music?
   d) What should your exciting girl/boy look like?
   e) Tell me another situation where you might be in high spirits.
   f) Start writing the letter all by yourself.
   g) When do you blush?
   h) What's the difference between grand balls and disco dancing?
   i) Why don't some people write letters any more?
   j) Which qualities must your future partner have?

3. Answer each further question in a sentence.
   a) Tell me something about the duties of the fire brigade.
   b) How can you support the fire brigade?
   c) Where are posters usually put up, where shouldn't you put them up?
   d) What's a date, what's a blind date?
   e) What must you do when you post a letter?
   f) What do nosy or curious people do?
   g) Why aren't children or even grown-ups delighted when mum or dad or a teacher or the boss wants to speak to them in private?
   h) When are parents, teachers, bosses angry?
   i) Some girls or boys say: "Don't fence me in." Tell me what it means.
   j) Why were young people, when they wanted to meet, dependent on the railway some thirty years ago? Which problems have arisen for the railway companies now? The post offices have got problems as well.

II. Translation

Translate and mind the "hidden" grammar.

1. Die Tür des Zuges öffnete sich nicht automatisch. Der Schaffner, um den sofort geschickt wurde, sollte sie öffnen.
2. Weder er noch ein Mechaniker konnten sie öffnen, aber dann ging sie plötzlich von selbst auf.
3. Da alle Fahrgäste gut gelaunt waren, tadelten sie den Schaffner dafür nicht.
4. Da unser junger Mann nicht im Wartesaal des Bahnhofs bleiben wollte, ging er auf den Feuerwehrball.
5. Verliebte er sich in das Mädchen, mit der er den Abend verbrachte? Warum konnte er nicht länger bleiben? Warum musste er das Mädchen verlassen?
6. Wie lange darfst du in der Disco sein? Früher durften die Mädchen oft nur auf einen Ball gehen, wenn sie eingeladen wurden. Seitdem die Discos aufgekommen sind, gibt es weniger Bälle.

7. "Du sollst dich gut benehmen!" "Ja, wir sollten uns auf dem Ball gut benehmen."
8. Gestern sollte er die Eintrittskarten für den Ball kaufen. Aber er musste sich auf die Englischschulaufgabe vorbereiten.
9. Falls du mich nicht für den Ball abholst, bin ich dir böse. Seit meinem 17. Geburtstag werde ich von dir abgeholt.
10. Falls du mich eher angerufen hättest, wäre ich nicht von deinem Bruder abgeholt worden.

III. Grammar

1. Translate, putting in the reflexive pronoun if possible.
   a) Ärgerte sich das Mädchen?
   b) Freute er sich über den Tanz?
   c) Interessierte er sich für sie?
   d) Vergnügte er sich?
   e) Er stellte sich nicht vor.

2. Translate, putting in the emphasizing pronoun.
   a) Bekam er den Brief selber?
   b) Die Beamten im Postamt öffneten den Brief selber.
   c) "Ich erinnere mich schon selber an den Ball."
   d) "Ja, ich verliebte mich, das kam ganz von selber."
   e) Das Mädchen denkt nur an sich selbst.

3. Translate, taking the reciprocal pronoun if possible.
   a) Die beiden sahen sich zum ersten Mal.
   b) Verliebten sie sich?
   c) Nein, sie stritten sich nicht.
   d) Ja, sie küssten sich.
   e) Sie schauten sich zärtlich an.

4. Translate and put into reported speech.
   a) Er sagt/hat gesagt/wird sagen: "Ich mag Bälle."
   b) Er sagt/hat gesagt/wird sagen: "Ich bevorzuge moderne Schlager."
   c) Er sagt/hat gesagt/wird sagen: "Ich muss versuchen, sie zu finden."
   d) Er sagt/hat gesagt/wird sagen: "Ich sollte sie eigentlich nicht suchen."
   e) Er sagt/hat gesagt/wird sagen: "Ich denke, sie darf ihn nicht sehen."

5. Put once again into reported speech.
   a) Er sagte/hatte gesagt/würde sagen: "Ich mag Bälle."
   b) Er sagte/hatte gesagt/würde sagen: "Ich bevorzuge moderne Schlager."
   c) Er sagte/hatte gesagt/würde sagen: "Ich muss versuchen, sie zu finden."
   d) Er sagte/hatte gesagt/würde sagen: "Ich sollte sie eigentlich nicht suchen."
   e) Er sagte/hatte gesagt/würde sagen: "Ich denke, sie darf ihn nicht sehen."

6. Reported questions: Report what he asks/has asked/will ask.
   a) He always asks/has asked/will ask: "What shall I do?"
   b) He always asks/has asked/will ask: "Where should I go?"
   c) He always asks/has asked/will ask: "Can you help me?"
   d) He always asks/has asked/will ask: "Could you support me?"
   e) He always asks/has asked/will ask: "Do you understand girls?"

7. Reported questions: Report what he asked/had asked/would ask.
   a) He asked/had asked/would ask: "What shall I do?"
   b) He asked/had asked/would ask: "Where should I go?"
   c) He asked/had asked/would ask: "Can you help me?"
   d) He asked/had asked/would ask: "Could you support me?"
   e) He asked/had asked/would ask: "Do you understand girls?"

8. Decide whether -ing or infinitive or both.
    a) I love (dance) ______________.
    b) I can't afford (attend) ________________ balls every week.
    c) I enjoy (dance) ______________.
    d) She didn't mind (give) _____________ a wrong address.
    e) He promised (write) ____________ a letter.

The Incident

St Michael's is the parish church. You don't know who St Michael is? He is the archangel who fought against evil and was therefore the patron saint of the medieval knights. The sacristan had to ring the church bells in the morning, my duty was to ring them in the evening. In winter it was rather dark and I was a bit scared of being alone in the church. After having rung the bells, I ran quickly back and locked the doors hastily. Once I read in the newspaper that criminals had stolen the statue of St Christopher. I was a bit surprised as I believed that the saints would stop such a robbery or theft, or that a lightning would strike those wicked persons.

Our parson who instructed us at school had a view of his own. Everybody is free, that's the genuine human quality, and therefore no saint would interfere. When a pupil lost his life in an accident – he didn't see the traffic sign, fell on the kerb and was injured so heavily that he died in hospital immediately after –, he insisted on the pupil's guilt and that heaven can't abolish the laws of nature. We had a long discussion about that.

The assembly of people in church is of course a solemn event, totally different from the life outside. You can't talk to your neighbour, jokes are forbidden, even flirts (aren't they?). You have to pay attention to the sermon, you can't interrupt or disturb. You may understand that everybody was shocked when a man of about forty attacked the parson, knocked him down and then wanted to leave the church, waving his hands furiously. But some brave men held him until the police came. Police Officer Peter Kitter had never heard of such an incident before. In a first questioning the man didn't give any plausible reason for his action. As the police psychologist talked to him, the man answered after hesitating some time that he was full of despair as he had lost his job and his wife wanted a divorce.

Let's finish our text with a story not so sad as the one above. Uncle Charles didn't like to confess his sins in the parish church as the parson and he knew each other very well. Therefore he went to the Benedictine Abbey fifty kilometres away. But he had reckoned without his host. As our parson stayed for some days in the abbey, he was sitting in the confessional and asked our penitent Charles: "Did you have a nice trip to this abbey, it is excellent weather, isn't it?"

Worksheet

I. Questions on the text

1. Answer each question on the text in a complete sentence.
   a) Why did the pupil not like ringing the bells in winter?
   b) Why was the pupil astonished to read that criminals had taken away the statue of St Christopher?
   c) Did the parson share the opinion of our pupil that saints should have stopped the robbery?
   d) Which passage shows you the pupils were not satisfied with the parson's explanations?
   e) Think of yourself and tell me why the pupils weren't satisfied.
   f) Everybody is shocked when he sees another person is being attacked. Why was it even more shocking that the incident was in the church?
   g) Say in your own words why the man was so desperate.
   h) Why did Uncle Charles go to the Benedictine Abbey?
   i) Why did he "reckon without his host"?
   j) In which way was our parson ironical?

2. Answer each additional question in a full sentence as well.
   a) Why do you think St Michael was the patron saint of the medieval knights?
   b) Why is it easier to ring the bells now than years ago?
   c) Our pupil noticed that the statue had been missing for some days but he didn't inform the parson or the sacristan. Why, do you think?
   d) Can you tell me anything about the laws of nature?
   e) What must you do if you are a witness of a crime?
   f) When are you desperate and what can you do about it?
   g) What's the job of a psychologist?
   h) Stories happening at school can't be so sad many pupils think. But ...
   i) Why do you think our parson stayed for some days in the abbey?
   j) Make a list of sins or wrongdoings or faults.

3. Answer each further question in a sentence.
   a) Unemployment is a big problem. Which other problems might be a burden for people?
   b) Tell me something about the reasons for unemployment.
   c) What are the consequences of it?
   d) Which problems might arise if you have a lot of children?
   e) Which problems might arise for parents when their children attend school?
   f) Is there any way of avoiding divorces?
   g) I know a lot of young people who don't want to marry. They simply live together. Can you tell me why?
   h) What are the disadvantages of such "trial marriages"?
   i) What are the consequences of divorce?
   j) You are a young pupil and you have doubtlessly realised that many things aren't ideal. Which is the worst problem for you?

II. Translation

Translate into English.

1. Der Mesner sagte, dass der heilige Michael der Patron der Pfarrkirche ist.
2. Werden die Kirchenglocken vom Ministranten oder vom Mesner geläutet? Sie werden seit einem Jahrzehnt sowohl vom Mesner als auch vom Ministranten geläutet.
3. Der Pfarrer belehrte uns intensiv über den freien Willen. Wir diskutierten tatsächlich lange über das Problem. Seit dieser Stunde beschäftigen wir uns mit dieser Sache.
4. Die Predigt wurde unterbrochen, glauben Sie mir! Der Mann konnte sich nicht beherrschen.
5. Er weigerte sich, die Kirche zu verlassen und sich zu entschuldigen.
6. Der Pfarrer ärgerte sich und fürchtete sich auch vor dem Mann. "Der Mann benimmt sich nicht," sagten die Leute.

7. Erinnert ihr euch an den Vorfall? Wisst ihr noch, wann sich der Vorfall ereignete?
8. Zuerst verliebten sie sich, dann stritten sie sich und trennten sich.
9. Sie sahen sich nie wieder, sie vertragen sich nicht mehr.
10. Ist das von allein gekommen? Der Mann hat selber keine Lösung gefunden.

III. Grammar

1. Put into reported speech.
   a) The man said: "I was full of despair."
   b) He said: "My wife will leave me."
   c) He said: "By next Sunday she will have left me."
   d) He said: "In earlier years she had never been unfaithful."
   e) He said: "She will move out of our flat tomorrow. I don't understand all these things."

2. Fill in the correct tense.
   a) Uncle Charles (live) ____________ in the town since 1960.
   b) He (never / be) ____________ to Africa (up to now) ____________.
   c) (already / see) ______________ the pyramids in Egypt (up to now) ____________?
   d) (ever / visit) ____________ the Benedictine Abbey in Buckfast?
   e) I am so sorry. I am so tired because I (just / arrive) ____________ here in the abbey.

3. Put into the passive.
   a) For one year the sacristan has rung the bells.
   b) Gangsters stole the statue of St Christopher.
   c) Since the incident they have held the man.
   d) They would question him all night if they had time.
   e) She wouldn't have moved out of the flat if ...

4. Translate into English.
   a) Die Sünden zu bekennen ist sicher lästig.
   b) Aber auch im Beichtstuhl sitzen ist anstrengend.
   c) Es macht gewiss keinen Spaß, die Nöte der Menschen anzuhören.
   d) Im Klostergarten spazieren zu gehen entspannt mich.
   e) Das fröhliche Gezwitscher der Vögel ist wie Musik.
   f) Die Patres singen gerade den Choral.
   g) Der Pater sagte: "Du vergisst immer, was du versprochen hast." Er sagte das ärgerlich.
   h) "Ich sage es zum letzten Mal", fürge er hinzu.
   i) Seit einer Stunde schreibt Pater Michael einen Aufsatz über den Gregorianischen Choral.
   j) Als er gestern Vormittag im Studierzimmer saß, rief der Bischof an.

5. Decide between "since" and "for".
   a) ________ May 4, 1996
   b) ________ Easter
   c) ________ 20 years
   d) ________ yesterday
   e) ________ a century

6. Agree "Ich auch (nicht)".
   a) "I sometimes talk to my neighbour."
   b) "I sometimes told jokes."
   c) "I have paid attention to the sermon."
   d) "I won't flirt in the church."
   e) "I don't like chatting people there myself."

The Car

We usually spent our holidays in Italy, sometimes in Switzerland. It seemed to us like a paradise. Above all, we liked the Lake of Garda and the town of Sirmione, which isn't a big town and almost all the hotels are surrounded by big parks where there are enough parking places. On the northern side of our hotel there was a big car park. There were two rows of parking lots on each side of a narrow "corridor" of gravel. The car shelters had corrugated iron roofs, resting on iron poles. The problem was to get into a parking space between these two iron rods. Another problem was that the parking lots weren't big, Italian cars are usually smaller. When I tried to get into such a space I hit an iron rod, and as I wasn't slow, the right rear door was damaged, not only light scratches on the paintwork, there was a big dent. What should be done? I reversed the car and parked near the hotel entrance.

Always maintaining I am the best driver in the world, I didn't dare to tell my wife. I wouldn't have stood her comments and the malicious joy. And of course she would have blamed me for having damaged the car. So I went straight to our room, number 13 (!), but didn't mention the incident.

We had dinner. Do you remember the tables in Italian hotels with the bottles of wine and mineral water and the different glasses upside down? Incidentally I began talking about the car, which was still in front of the hotel entrance and had to be parked in the car park. "I don't think, I can do that after I've drunk some glasses of wine. I am not accustomed to such a quantity of wine – my apologies: The first day in Italy."

After dinner I went into the hotel bar and my wife wanted to park the car. After some minutes she came back, rather pale, started to talk: "Sweet-heart ..." – an alarming term indeed; she must have noticed the dent! Alas!. "Sweetheart, there is a big dent in the driver's door. I have knocked into one of those damned iron rods."

Then it was my turn to confess my sin. After coming home from the holiday, I went to my garage to have the two doors repaired. The full team and the foreman laughed about the story. Then they put my car on the platform to raise it. But because of all the laughter and the rather funny situation the workman had forgotten to close the left rear door. Suddenly we heard a crunching noise when that door hit an iron pole. The foreman pressed the stop knob, but it was too late. Door number 3 ...

Worksheet

I. Questions on the text

1. Answer each question on the text in a complete sentence.
   a) What is the principal advantage for motorists when they go to smaller towns?
   b) Tell me the two reasons why it was difficult to get into the parking lots.
   c) Why didn't our motorist tell his wife about the mishap?
   d) Why did our vacationist drink a lot of wine that evening?
   e) What was he afraid of when his wife began addressing him "Sweet-heart"?
   f) Why was he no longer afraid of telling his wife what he had done?
   g) Why couldn't our vacationist's wife blame her husband any more?
   h) Why did the foreman and the other workmen laugh about it?
   i) Why did one workman forget to close the left rear door?
   j) Why was the foreman's reaction too late?

2. Answer each additional question in a full sentence as well.
   a) Say in your own words why they usually spent their holidays in Italy. Don't copy the text.
   b) What is the difference between Italy and Switzerland? Write down three items each.
   c) Why are there car shelters?
   d) Why do you think Italian cars are normally smaller?
   e) When do you feel any malicious joy?
   f) Some hotels leave number 13 out. Why do you think the motorist or vacationist mentioned that number?
   g) What might the holiday-maker have been thinking when he was waiting for his wife in the hotel bar?
   h) Where can you confess your sins or faults?
   i) Why did they have to raise the platform?
   j) Where else must you press knobs or buttons?

3. Answer each further question in a sentence.
   a) What must you do when you want to slow down?
   b) What must you do when you want to overtake a tractor, a lorry, another motor vehicle?
   c) Check your car before leaving.
   d) Tell me four things which are absolutely forbidden when steering a car.
   e) Why shouldn't you hitch-hike?
   f) Some people want to ban cars. Write down items in favour of the car.
   g) But environmentalists say that the car ...
   h) In which way can the number of accidents be reduced?
   i) Why is the automobile industry vital for the nation's economy?
   j) Write down four parts of the car and what they are for.

II. Translation

Translate and mind the "hidden" grammar.

1. Der Gardasee, den sie gerne mögen, ist der schönste See Italiens, behauptet unser Ehepaar, das oft dorthin fährt.
2. Das Hotel, in dem sie die Nächte verbringen, ist weniger laut als andere.
3. "Sieh dir diese wunderschöne Landschaft an", sagt der Mann immer zu seiner Frau.
4. Auch die Möbel im Hotelzimmer sind moderner als in den anderen Hotels.
5. Bevor sie einen Ausflug machen, studieren sie viele Prospekte und Landkarten.
6. Sie duschen sich immer, nachdem sie im Meer geschwommen sind.
7. Da sie das italienische Essen mögen, freuen sie sich immer auf das Abendessen.
8. Sobald sie den Speisesaal betreten, sind sie glücklich.

9. Sie wünschen, dass wir sie einmal im Hotel besuchen. Da wir aber lieber nach Norwegen fahren, wünschte ich, sie würden uns nicht einladen.

10. Gestern riefen sie an und fragten, ob wir nächste Woche kommen würden.

III. Grammar

1. Translate into English.
   a) Die Möbel im Hotelzimmer waren modern.
   b) Im Urlaub trägt sie nur elegante Jeans.
   c) "Ich will diese Jeans kaufen, Signorina."
   d) "Eine Delle am Auto. Das ist keine gute Information. Es gibt bessere Informationen, in der Tat."
   e) "Du hast doch eine neue Brille! Das ist eine schlechte Nachricht!"

2. Put into reported speech.
   a) The man said: "The car must be repaired."
   b) The man said: "I would suggest Mayor's garage."
   c) The man said: "By next Wednesday Mr Mayor will have repaired my car."
   d) The man said: "If he had had the materials he would have repaired it by next Monday."
   e) The man said: "It should be repaired, indeed!"

3. Translate into English.
   a) "Es hätte schlimmer kommen können."
   b) "Ich hätte einen Unfall haben können."
   c) "Du hättest aber aufpassen können."
   d) "Auch du hättest aufpassen sollen."
   e) "Ich muss den Pfosten nicht gesehen haben."

4. Put into reported statements, questions and orders.
   a) He asked: "Where is the car now?"
   b) He said: "Ring Mr Mayor."
   c) He said: "Everybody can make a mistake."
   d) He asked: "By which day will the car have been repaired?"
   e) He asked: "Should the car be repaired at all or is it better for me to buy a new car?"

5. Translate into English.
   a) Gestern habe ich den Meister getroffen.
   b) Sahst du ihn bereits?
   c) Seit 1960 arbeitete er in einem Hotel, dann machte er eine Lehre als Mechaniker; seit 1975 arbeitet er bei Mr Mayor.
   d) Er versprach mir, dass der Wagen bis zum Mittwoch repariert sei.
   e) Er sagte auch, dass, wenn er das Material gehabt hätte, er ihn schon eher hätte reparieren können.

6. Translate the wishes.
   a) Wir wollen wieder nach Italien fahren.
   b) Ich will aber, dass nur du fährst.
   c) Es wäre aber auch schön, wenn du mir einen Zweitwagen schenken würdest.
   d) Ich wünschte, ich hätte in der Lotterie gewonnen.
   e) Wenn ich nur in der Lotterie gewonnen hätte!

Keys

The Sparrow or How to Treat Animals

I. Questions on the text

1. a) They didn't find a proper restaurant.

   b) The waitress was young and neat. His wife wasn't happy as she didn't like her husband's joking with the young girl.
   Hinweis: nach *like* auch *-ing*-Form mit besitzanzeigendem *s*-Genitiv

   c) It wasn't good for his health as he was suffering from heart attacks and a severe diabetes.

   d) His wife didn't see it, the young waitress smiled as every girl is glad about compliments.

   e) Mr Joule suffered from heart attacks and an accident might have been the consequence.

   f) Mr Joule saw an ancient tower and was a fan of history. She didn't like that old stuff.

   g) It simply wanted to escape and fly away and it wanted to escape Mr Joule as well.

   h) The heart of the sparrow was as it was flying continuously and Mr Joule's was as he was chasing the bird.
   Hinweis: Hier ist die Verlaufsform vorzuziehen, weil der Vorgang lang dauert.

   i) He was happy as he was able to catch it and let it out in the open air. If he hadn't been able to catch it the bird would have starved in the tower.
   Hinweis: *it* beachten; Bedingungssatz: 3. Vergangenheit + 2. Bedingungsform

   j) She might have thought of a heart attack as her husband didn't return.

2. a) You shouldn't eat eggs, fatty sausages, any fat meat or any liver, kidney and so on. Mind your cholesterol level and the promotion of arteriosclerosis; as for diabetes: You oughtn't to eat chocolate, or

even a box of chocolate, too much bread, cakes and so on. You must restrict yourself to special food and live on a strict diet and eat diabetic food.

b) You should eat salads, vegetables, lean meat e. g. veal; you should drink mineral water; the diabetic ought to eat special food and drink mineral water as well.

c) He isn't just a womanizer (he isn't unfaithful) but he likes seeing the other sex especially the "younger variety".

d) A waiter or waitress is a person who serves food and drinks in a restaurant. You give a big tip when the waiter is very friendly and attentive or a young girl (Mr Joule gives a lot then).

Hinweis: *who serves* auch verkürzt: *serving*

e) I guess she was a bit angry with her husband as he was joking with the waitress or she noticed that he was waving his hands.

f) She usually read detective stories.

g) She should have accompanied him as he suffered from heart attacks and was chasing the bird.

h) A bird is quicker or flies more quickly than a person can run. A bird is rather small.

Hinweis: Umstandsangabe, Steigerung immer mit *more*, unabhängig von der Silbenzahl des Grundworts; nur Ausnahmefall z. B. *fast, hard: faster, harder ...*; auch Superlativ: *the bird was flying most quickly,* aber *fastest*.

i) He likes birds, they are so sweet, so tiny.

j) Usually birds fly upwards in a building or staircase and not downwards.

3. a) Animals are creatures which feel the same pain as people and they are truly helpless and at the mercy of people.

b) I can enter a society for the protection of animals, I can write letters to politicians, letters to the editor of a newspaper or magazine, I can take part in a demonstration.

c) It's simply cruel and the transport should be abolished at once.

d) It cannot, as animals are born and if we don't slaughter them they will be bound to die by themselves.

e) It's a big problem. On the one hand we need experiments to find medicine or remedies against disease or illness, on the other hand it's cruel. We should reduce the experiments and try to find other ways. Nevertheless experiments because of cosmetics should be banned.

f) **For:** You aren't lonely, you have got a sort of companion, it helps you to forget all the stress, it can guard your house, children can play with it.
Against: There is some inconvenience because of food and the toilet, some pets like scratching the couch or the carpet, if you go on holiday you must find a person who looks after it.

g) I think there are far too many cats there and therefore your cat must be castrated.

h) It is to be recommended as the old people aren't so lonely and if they are ill they will recover more quickly as psychologists and doctors have found out.

i) It's because of rabies. The United Kingdom doesn't want to "import" this disease.

j) It's a disease especially of cows which can be transferred to people who die from the so-called Creutzfeldt-Jakob-Disease, when they have eaten BSE-infected meat. The correct scientific name is BSE for Bovine Spongiform Encephalopathy. CJD is very rare indeed and I hope you won't be compelled to answer this question in the years to come.

II. Translation

1. In which season are the little birds grateful, if you are a generous host(ess)?
2. Mr Joule had pleasure in watching his "guests" in the garden.
   Hinweis: in dieser Verbindung Hauptwort und Verhältniswort nur *-ing*
3. Undoubtedly I am responsible for them, especially in a rough winter.

4. Last summer I succeeded in freeing a sparrow on account of my interest in history.
   Hinweis: in dieser Verbindung Zeitwort + Verhältniswort nur *-ing*

5. I didn't give up chasing the sparrow and I didn't mind running for some time.
   Hinweis: Zeitwort + Verhältniswort + *-ing; to mind* immer + *-ing*

6. For many years I have been convinced that you shouldn't lock up animals (our sparrow had actually locked up itself).
   Hinweis: "seit" + 2. Vergangenheit; das betonende Fürwort *oneself*, hier *itself*

7. If the sparrow had had an escape route, he would have escaped from me.
   Hinweis: Bedingungssatz, 3. Muster: 3. Vergangenheit + 2. Bedingungsform

8. Apart from numerous publications I support the protection of animals with occasional lectures.

9. Since 1960 he has influenced public opinion.
   Hinweis: "seit" + 2. Vergangenheit

10. He admits being proud of it.
    Hinweis: *to admit* + *-ing*

III. Grammar

1. a) seeing

   b) him talking to/his talking to
   Hinweis: entweder persönliches Fürwort im Objekt oder besitzanzeigendes Fürwort

   c) to chase/chasing

   d) to catch

   e) to go

2. a) on her husband ordering/her husband's ordering
   Hinweis: vergleiche dazu oben 1 b

   b) for flirting

   c) from eating

d) for being

e) on her helping him
Hinweis: Nach dem Verhältniswort steht immer *-ing!*

3. a) to have

b) of visiting/to visit

c) for eating/to eat

d) of getting

e) of chatting

4. a) drank

b) have made

c) have preferred
Hinweis: gemeint ist "seit ... bis jetzt"

d) will travel

e) is studying
Hinweis: Verlaufsform der Gegenwart; möglich wäre natürlich noch: ... *has just studied ...*

5. a) Mrs Joule drives/is driving herself.

b) The sparrow couldn't free itself.

c) Mr Joule freed it himself.

d) In the restaurant Mr Joule wasn't allowed/permitted to order himself.

e) "I take care of him myself."

6. a) will become
Hinweis: Modell 1: *if*-Satz Gegenwart, Hauptsatz 1. Zukunft mit *will*

b) would have starved
Hinweis: Modell 3: *if*-Satz 3. Vergangenheit, Hauptsatz 2. Bedingungsform, *would have* + Mittelwort der Verg.

c) hadn't come
Hinweis: auch Modell 3

d) ate

Hinweis: Modell 2: *if*-Satz 1. Verg., Hauptsatz 1. Bedingungsform, *would*

e) doesn't take

Hinweis: Sonderform 1: *if*-Satz Gegenwart, Hauptsatz Hilfszeitwort Gegenwart

Uncle Charles or How to Educate Children

I. Questions on the text

1. a) You needn't read the text if your parents aren't any problem.

   b) His dad was a soldier and was killed in World War II. When Charles was born his dad was already dead.

   c) He thinks it was the wrong way. She often confused little Charles. He was afraid of being alone. He was desperate and cried.

   d) He thinks the readers of the text will educate their children in a better way.

   e) She was against it because she didn't want to lose her Charles. It was simply a pretence. If he had got to know the wealthiest girl she would have been against marrying as well.

   f) A typically Italian "mamma" does everything for her son and controls his life thoroughly.

   g) He was a genuine "mammista", living with "mamma", and even spending the holidays with her.

   h) The trick was no longer effective as the lady was a doctor and not a shop assistant or a nurse or a guide.

   i) She didn't look content first because she was simply against the marriage. That she kissed her son and even her daughter-in-law shows that she yielded to the new facts.

   j) She consoled herself with two pieces of cream cake and two glasses of sherry.

2. a) A resolute person is someone who always wants to do/wants you to do what he/she wants. If you don't he/she will get furious.

   Hinweis: Definitionen sind immer "notwendige" Nebensätze, deshalb auch ... *someone always wanting*

   b) I think dads are vital for one's education as nature has established that. If there is no dad some other male person might play the part.

c) I was totally desperate and sad when I was lost in a big forest at night and couldn't find the way back or when I lost my mum in a big store.

d) I think it's cruel to treat animals in a way they feel pain or to hit children and to mistreat them./Treating children and babies badly is unbearable.

e) I would try to convince them without any tricks. I would be consistent and not change my principles. I wouldn't do anything which makes the child desperate.

f) Apart from a doctor (she had to accept it) I can think of a teacher, a professor, a lawyer, a scientist.

g) "Mama" needn't be afraid of "losing" him.

h) I am jealous if my partner is happy when some other person is there, if my partner always hesitates to dance with me but is happy to dance with some other person. If it is an addiction call a psychologist.

i) It was a detour or deviation as the lady doctor lived in the same town. Why the deviation via Italy then?

j) I must yield to my parents, teachers, lack of money.

3. a) There is crime. People are robbed and killed, kidnapped and hurt. Girls and women are raped. There are wars with a lot of victims. There are rich people who don't know how to spend their money and there are poor people. What can I do about that? I am not allowed to give up and must work for a better world.

b) World War II lasted from 1939 to 1945. First the German army invaded Poland. Then Germany and its allies waged war with the Soviet Union, Great Britain, the United States and so on. Millions of soldiers and civilians lost their lives. Germany was defeated.

c) There you can have a fine dinner and drink exclusive wines. A music band plays. The guests give presents to the young couple. Some guests dance.

d) It means "Good lord", "Oh dear".

e) I simply want to go to Italy because of the warm climate. It rarely rains there. There are sandy beaches. I can relax by wind surfing.

f) Possibly it's cheaper, the weather isn't as bad, they think they can relax better in quite a different area.

g) Visit Bavaria. Fascinating scenery! Lakes and mountains, King Ludwig's castles, palaces are there, the typically Bavarian food is super, enjoy the Bavarian beer, it's so cosy in Bavaria.

h) In Italy or France and England you can't simply go to a table and sit down. You have to ask the waiter where to sit.

i) You are exhausted and need relaxation.

j) It's a problem indeed. Experts say it's only a short romance and causes lots of troubles. Just think of the dangers to your health.

II. Translation

1. Do you know many "mammas" who don't want their sons to be "carried away"?

   Hinweis: *to want* + Objekt + Infinitiv vorgeschrieben; in unserem Fall Infinitiv des Passivs

2. In view of the fact that they lose the connection with their sons, they want to stop the "romance" as a rule.

3. She couldn't help continually watching the girl with whom her son was dancing.

   Hinweis: *couldn't help* + *-ing*; auch *who her son was dancing with ...*

4. After she had overturned the glass of wine intentionally, she left the café furiously.

   Hinweis: der Zeitnebensatz auch: *After having overturned .../Having overturned .../After overturning*; Umstandsangaben: Wie ...?

5. The son had to stop dancing and to negotiate with the waiter.

   Hinweis: *had to* hier die beste Form, *was forced* ist zu stark

6. The young lady: "You are to become independent."

   Hinweis: andere Wendungen für "sollen": *are expected to, supposed to, told to; you are said to* passt nicht (Man sagt es von ...)

7. She remarked, smilingly: "You ought to entertain me now."
   Hinweis: anstatt *ought to* auch *should*

8. As he didn't worry about his "mamma" and relied on her returning, he had time to talk to the young lady.
   Hinweis: anstatt *as* auch *because;* auch verkürzen zu *Not worrying about his ...*; *rely + on* immer mit *-ing*; das Fürwort *she* wird als besitzanzeigendes Fürwort vorangestellt: *her*.

9. "Mamma" had stayed in the cloakroom before she went to the bus stop.
   Hinweis: Verkürzung: *before going to ...*

10. She had gone home totally unexpectedly.
    Hinweis: doppelte Umstandsangabe: Wie war sie nach Hause gefahren? Wie unerwartet war sie nach Hause gefahren?

III. Grammar

1. a) Charles invited the shop assistant to go with him to the pictures.

   b) Her friend encouraged her to accept the invitation.

   c) For a long time he has wanted her to accompany him.

   d) "Can I rely on you to go with me, Caroline?"

   e) "I would like them to show films only with Humphrey Bogart at the cinema."

   Hinweis: bei einem bestimmten Zeitwort immer Objekt + Infinitiv; Satz c: 2. Vergangenheit, da sinngemäß "bis jetzt"

2. a) to be invited

   b) to be collected

   c) being kissed

   Hinweis: a–c immer Leideform!

   d) meeting her

   e) buying

3. a) Who is the girl with whom you talked/... were talking/... who you talked to/... that you talked to/... the girl you talked to?

b) The girl with whom he danced/...was dancing is called Cissy/... girl who he danced with .../... girl that he danced with .../... girl he danced with ...

c) I mean the honeymoon which they spent in Venice/... that they spent .../... honeymoon they spent ...

d) The girl whom he always invites is called Catherine/... that he .../... girl he always invites ...

e) The hotel in which they spent the honeymoon is at the sea/... hotel which they spent their honeymoon in .../... hotel that they spent their honeymoon in .../... hotel they spent their honeymoon in ...

Hinweis: Die letzteren Möglichkeiten (mit nachgestelltem Verhältniswort) sind immer die sprachlich elegantesten.

4. a) After having met .../Having met .../After meeting ...

b) After having written .../Having written .../After writing ...

c) Before posting it ...

d) On getting a letter ...

e) Before opening ...

Hinweis: *before* schafft keine Probleme; es spielt ebenfalls keine Rolle, in welcher Zeit der *after*-Satz steht, da immer alle drei Varianten richtig sind.

5. a) happily

b) quick, fast

c) fast

d) especially slowly, fast

e) wittily, in a friendly way

Hinweis: Grundsätzlich *-ly* nach der Frage wie?; *fast* ist eine Ausnahme; doppelte Umstandsangabe: Wie arbeitet er? Wie langsam arbeitet er? (nicht mit der Tür ins Haus fallen!); Schreibung bei *y*! Ist bereits eine *-ly*-Endung da, dann "umschreiben": *in a ... way/manner*

6. a) Charles said that he had to/was compelled/obliged/forced to dance with her.

b) Charles said that she wasn't allowed to/permitted to go out.

c) Charles said she had to/was compelled to/obliged to/forced to be there.

d) Charles said that she was allowed/was permitted to visit him that day.

e) Charles said that she was able to cook well/could cook well.

Hinweis: a–e: Das berichtende Zeitwort steht in der 1. Vergangenheit, *past,* deshalb notwendige "Verschiebungen" des Hilfszeitworts. Das Hilfszeitwort *must* kann in der indirekten Rede nicht "verschoben" werden, bei *may* ist *might* möglich, bei *can* auch *could.* Letztere sind keine Vergangenheitsformen, sie dürfen nur bei der indirekten Rede genommen werden. Sinngemäß sind auch Zeitangaben zu verändern, da sie nicht mehr stimmen.

7. a) "You should telephone now."

Hinweis: in der Gegenwart nur *should* oder *ought to*

b) She was to visit us .../she was expected to .../she was supposed to .../ she was told to visit us yesterday.

Hinweis: in der Vergangenheit verschiedene Möglichkeiten, der Sinn ist natürlich verschieden; die "stärkste" Form: *was to visit*; *expected*, man erwartete es; *supposed*, man vermutete es; *told*, man befahl es

c) What am I to do?/What am I expected to do?/What am I supposed to do?/What am I told to do?

d) You were to marry/You were expected to marry. Why didn't you get married?

Hinweis: Sinngemäß ist Vergangenheit gemeint.

e) He is said to often spend the holidays in Italy.

Hinweis: Im Hinblick auf das oben Gesagte ist *to be said* am besten: man sagt es allgemein von ihm.

8. a) "Mamma" being against the marriage, they couldn't get married.

b) Preferring blondes, I'm not interested in you.

c) Having met Cissy, I don't want to see you any more.

d) Being invited to the party, I didn't have time.

e) Having been picked up by Charles, she couln't help liking him.

Hinweis: c + e Vorzeitigkeit, einmal Tatform, einmal Leideform; d ebenfalls Leideform

How to Find Missing Members

I. Questions on the text

1. a) It is an ancient town with walls and ditches. There are more visitors at weekends as they needn't work and have got time.

   b) The town has become a modern industrial town with a lot of factories and offices and increasing traffic.

   c) There are many plants or factories, high office buildings, there are smoking chimneys. There is a high level of air pollution, but not necessarily, as you can use filters or simply do what the laws to protect the environment want you to do or not respectively.

   d) A lot of pedestrian zones have been established and only a few one-way roads cross the ancient city.

   e) The car parks are on the periphery of the ancient city. The council had the ditches simply filled up.

   Hinweis: "Der Stadtrat ließ die Gräben auffüllen." (er machte es nicht selber: *have* + Objekt + Vergangenheitsmittelwort)

   f) They were undoubtedly not right as the chairman had informed them with the microphone where they were and when to come back.

   g) He had soon realised that he was at the wrong car park and then he went by bus.

   h) I think he was amused as usually a person wants to get to somewhere by taxi and doesn't try to discover a missing person.

   i) Everything occurred rather quickly. Usually a kidnapped person is pushed into a car.

   j) There was more than one car park on the periphery and logically they might have all looked alike.

2. a) A lot of people go to work by car or go home by car again. A lot of lorries take material to the plants and factories, other commercial cars collect products to take them to the shops. The increase in traffic is not only due to industry. It is an ancient town with historic buildings and I think there are a lot of stores and excellent restaurants and pubs.

b) The owners of shops think fewer people can get to their shops and stores. And there are people who are unable to walk more than one hundred metres. Or don't the pedestrian zones look rather deserted, especially on Sundays?

c) I think they were ashamed of themselves and didn't want the author to publish their names in a book. Apart from that, they had to bear some making fun of them.

d) They were doubtful whether the chairman or the treasurer would be able to find the two other missing members because the town was rather big with a lot of inhabitants and vacationists and excursionists and it was indeed a big coincidence.

e) You can take a taxi if your car is in the garage or the police have confiscated your driving licence or you haven't got a licence at all and no car.

f) He gets to know a lot of people from film stars to spleeny people, from fascinating people to interesting ones.

g) They might have made fun of them. "Hello, haven't you found a hotel to stay in the town, have you?" "You have always been cleverer than the rest of us (at least in your opinion)." " Good Lord, you are here, it's too early."

h) She might have thought her husband had had a severe heart attack and was in hospital or even dead.

i) I am so sorry. I didn't understand what the chairman said on the bus. I didn't hear the information he gave as the other passengers were too loud. I simply didn't find the way back.

j) "You needn't hurry, we have got a lot of time."

3. a) They aren't vital any more. In the Middle Ages they had to keep enemies or criminals out. Modern enemies can surpass the walls with their modern arms (think of firearms, tanks, aircraft, missiles). The towns are too big now to surround them with walls or fences, the new lifestyle with people going out till midnight or even longer makes walls and ditches useless. We've got an open society.

b) They read a lot of historical books and documents in the archives, visit ancient towns with famous palaces and cathedrals and so on.

c) There are a lot of don'ts: If possible I shouldn't go by car and use a public means of transport instead, or a bike or I ought to walk; my car should have a catalyst (catalytic converter); use gas instead of oil for my heating; I must save energy; I can/must buy articles which can be recycled; I don't buy tins, it's better to buy glass bottles which can be given back or bottles which have a deposit; I don't throw away litter; I put my rubbish into different rubbish bins; in my private environment I don't smoke and so on.

d) In a one-way street there is logically less traffic than in a street of two or more lanes.

e) The society wants an increase in historical research and to further the interest in history and the past. There are meetings with talks and excursions. The society or club intends to encourage people to work in the archives or at least to collect and store historical things. Such a club publishes yearbooks and is eager to have the monuments of a town protected and not knocked down by "modernists".

f) Their intentions are not to spoil our environment by carelessness and egoism. They intend to influence the politicians and authorities, they demonstrate if necessary.

g) The consequences are e. g. acid rain, the destruction of our forests, polluted air and water, dangers to our health, deformities, new and unknown diseases and allergies.

h) The most friendly means of transport is the bicycle but it doesn't meet the requirements of the modern world. I think buses and trains are a friendly means of transport as they can convey a lot of people. Think of the energy: If they are driven by electricity the better (or solar cells).

i) They want to see new things, they want to spend a day with nice people, they simply wish to relax.

j) A coach is used for trips and excursions whereas a bus is a passenger-carrying motor vehicle which goes on a fixed route and has usually got a number.

II. Translation

1. For one year the members of the club have intended to go on a day excursion.

   Hinweis: "seit" + bestimmte Zeit = *for;* dieses *for* verlangt immer das *present perfect; to intend* zieht entweder den Infinitiv oder die *-ing*-Form nach sich; es ginge auch *intended going on*

2. They like to go to ancient towns and they don't mind going on long trips in coaches.

   Hinweis: auch *like going*; aber immer *mind* + *-ing*

3. A lot of them could even afford to stay in another town for several days, as/because they are already pensioners.

   Hinweis: auch *afford staying;* den Nebensatz kann man verkürzen, nämlich: *Being pensioners, a lot of them ...* (notwendige Umstellung)

4. They admit being interested in history and always feel like visiting historic towns.

   Hinweis: *admit* und *feel like* immer *-ing*

5. I also would like to make a trip, but usually I don't manage to decide where to go.

   Hinweis: zusammengefasst: Ein bestimmtes Zeitwort (a) kann den Infinitiv (*to* ...) nach sich ziehen, ein anderes (b) das sogenannte Gerund, die *-ing*-Form, ein drittes Zeitwort (c) erlaubt beides. a: *would like, to want, promise* ... b: *enjoy, dislike, give up* ... c: *start, continue, afford* ... (siehe die übrigen Aufgaben!)

6. The lady to whom I am just talking is the manager of the travel agency. (She is the most charming person I know).

   Hinweis: Der Vorschlag ist nicht so elegant, besser ist: *who/that I am talking to; the lady I am talking to;* bei diesem notwendigen Nebensatz (welche Dame?) die letzteren Verkürzungen bevorzugen!; das zweisilbige *charming* verlangt *more.* Dieses zweisilbige Eigenschaftswort hat nicht die Endsilbe(n) *-er, le* nach Mitlaut, *y, ow;* somit *easier,* aber *more famous;* somit *narrower;* zu *le: simpler,* aber *more fertile.*

7. The magazine which I have been reading for one year deals with interesting travels.

   Hinweis: anstatt *which* auch *that* oder ganz weglassen: *... magazine I have been reading ...*; 2. Vergangenheit bei "seit"

8. The only book in which my girl-friend is interested is the cookbook, but she is the worst cook in the world.

   Hinweis: anstatt *book in which ...* besser *book my girl-friend is interested in* oder *which my girl-friend is interested in ...* ; vergleiche auch *bad – worse – worst*

9. If you see my girl-friend, don't ask her why the taxi-driver always eats secretly in the restaurant.
   Hinweis: Bedingungssatz mit Befehlssatz in der Gegenwart; Umstandsangabe auf *-ly*

10. If two excursionists get into my car again in order to look for a lost member I will say proudly that I am an expert.
    Hinweis: Bedingungssatz 1: *if* Gegenwart, Hauptsatz Zukunft

III. Grammar

1. a) have gone

   b) have visited
   Hinweis: sinngemäß auch "seit", "bis jetzt"

   c) had departed
   Hinweis: 3. Vergangenheit

   d) am going to announce
   Hinweis: "beabsichtigte" Zukunft

   e) will be fine
   Hinweis: unbeeinflusste Zukunft

2. a) to speak/speaking

   b) to announce/announcing

   c) to come back

   d) seeing
   Hinweis: *to* hier Verhältniswort

   e) being
   Hinweis: *-ing* nach Verhältniswort wohl selbstverständlich!

3. a) Not finding the way back two members were rather nervous.

   b) Being rather angry, the chairman didn't tell any jokes as he usually did.
   Hinweis: *chairman* darf nicht verlorengehen

   c) Before telling the driver to start he counted his members.

d) Do you remember the members lost in the town?

e) In the ancient town there were many tourists looking for a proper restaurant.

Hinweis: d) ist Leideform, deshalb Mittelwort der Vergangenheit; e) ist Tatform, deshalb Mittelwort der Gegenwart.

4. a) The guide that the tourists/guide the tourists like best gets a prize from the mayor.

   b) The guide who the members listened to/that the members listened to/the guide the members listened to is one of the best.

   c) Can you tell me the excursion which everybody looks forward to?/... that everybody looks forward to ...?/... excursion everybody looks forward to?

   d) Is that the trip which the treasurer is reponsible for?/... that the treasurer is responsible for?/... trip the treasurer is responsible for?

   e) The last trip was the best that they ever had./... best they ever had.

5. a) worst

   b) worse

   c) most boring

   d) more amusing

   e) simplest

   Hinweis: das Eigenschaftswort *bad, worse, worst;* zweisilbiges *boring* zu *more boring* und *most boring,* da es nicht auf *-er, -le* nach Mitlaut, *-y* und *-ow* endet, also *cleverer, simpler, easier* und *narrower;* die Steigerung auf *more* und *most* wird immer üblicher, sogar bei einsilbigen Eigenschaftswörtern, etwa *more strict* anstatt *stricter, most strict* anstatt *strictest;* nur umgekehrt geht es nicht; dreisilbig immer *more* und *most, more amusing, most amusing.*

6. a) would have been

   Hinweis: 3. Muster: *if*-Satz 3. Vergangenheit, Hauptsatz 2. Bedingungsform

   b) wouldn't look

   Hinweis: 2. Muster: *if*-Satz 1. Vergangenheit, Hauptsatz 1. Bedingungsform

   c) forbids

   Hinweis: Befehlssatz Gegenwart, *if*-Satz Gegenwart

d) will get annoyed

Hinweis: 1. Muster: *if*-Satz Gegenwart, Hauptsatz 1. Zukunft

e) will be cancelled

Hinweis: 1. Muster, Hauptsatz Passiv

7. a) extremely

Hinweis: Wie wütend war er?, äußerst wütend, deshalb *extremely*

b) more quickly

Hinweis: eine Umstandsangabe immer mit *more* (und *most)* steigern, ganz gleich welche Silbenlänge außer *fast, hard: faster, harder*

c) happy

Hinweis: nach *look,* aussehen ohne *-ly,* wie auch bei *taste, sound, smell* und *seem*

d) bad

Hinweis: nach *feel* kein *-ly*

e) fluently / badly

Hinweis: in beiden Fällen: wie? keine Ausnahme

8. a) The chairman told us to return in time.

Hinweis: indirekter Befehl mit *to* (oder *not to*); die "Angesprochenen" können auch andere sein: *them, me, you* oder *the members, the excursionists; say* zu *tell*

b) The chairman told us not to be late.

c) The chairman said (that) we would visit the fortress.

Hinweis: *we would visit* ... je nach Sinn auch *they, you* ...

d) The chairman said (that) he had never seen that building.

e) The chairman said (that) they had to hurry then.

Hinweis: Bekanntlich verschiebt sich die Gegenwart in die 1. Vergangenheit, die 1. und die 2. Vergangenheit in die 3., die 1. Zukunft in die 1. Bedingungsform. Sinngemäß verändert sich *this* zu *that, now* zu *then.*

How to Get a Son-in-Law

I. Questions on the text

1. a) In the Stone Age man made all the things himself, in the following ages there was an increasing specialisation into different crafts.

   b) It's better to go out with another person instead of dining quite alone. It's safer for a lady if she is accompanied when going back to the hotel. There is the danger of being harassed or even attacked.

   c) Absolutely necessary is: Getting the mail out of the letterbox; putting the dustbin on the pavement; pulling down the blinds at night.

   d) He wasn't permitted to smoke or to consume the wines, cognacs, and he wasn't allowed to have girls in.

   e) The doorbell often rang because various people delivered newspapers and magazines or wished to sell something.

   f) She stuttered as she was totally amazed when a young man she had never seen before opened the front door.

   g) It really was. It wasn't the usual way of getting to know each other.

   h) The homesitter and the girl each realized that the other person was nice and charming.

   i) I think everybody would pass out if he or she returned from holiday and saw that the homesitter and the daughter had opened the front door together and were holding hands!

   j) They liked each other very much, they fell in love, holding hands.

2. a) An ancestor is a person who lived a long time ago; you are descended from him; we are all descended from Adam and Eve!

   b) A house has got more storeys or floors, a flat has only got one level in a block of flats naturally.

   c) They must be cleaned and aired because if they aren't, the air will be rather close and the dirt and dust will increase and there will be an unpleasant smell.

   d) I must water the plants so that they don't dry up.

e) I didn't complete my list in the story. I think you must also check the heating, the water supply of the dishwasher or washing machine, the roof after heavy rainfall.

f) Smoking was forbidden as our family didn't like smoking at all and the smell of smoke was terrible and the smell will get into the curtains. Our homesitter must do his job well and therefore he isn't allowed to drink. I think alcoholic drinks are expensive, too.

g) I usually begin to stutter when I am very nervous or shocked or surprised.

h) My wife, Mrs ... (no name, private matter) passed out. The author is male as he tells us about his wife.

i) They say there isn't any love at first sight, as any characteristic of the other person you like is only a "duplicate" of another person's features you liked in your childhood. More simply: It might be the voice of your dad or favourite aunt.

j) It is indeed because it is the first step towards liking a person at once. If this is not the case you aren't interested in that person.

3. a) I can mention the Bronze Age, the Iron Age, the Ancient World, the Middle Ages, Modern History, the Atomic Age. In the Bronze Age they made tools and weapons of bronze, i. e. a mixture of copper and tin. They made tools and weapons of iron in the Iron Age, i. e. the Celtic Age as well. The Ancient World is the history of the Greeks and Romans, of philosophers such as Plato and emperors such as Augustus and Constantine. The Middle Ages is the Holy Roman Empire, reigned by the German emperors such as Otto the Great, the period of castles and knights. The Middle Ages end with the invention of firearms and Martin Luther's Reformation and Modern History begins with the discovery of America. The Atomic Age begins with the splitting of the nucleus and the use of atomic power. Some people say we're in the Computer Age now.

b) It is still increasing as the modern world has new needs which require specialists with special skills.

c) The rate of crime is increasing more and more such as murder, kidnapping, theft and robbery.

d) He must be a reliable person you can trust totally. He shouldn't steal anything or read your private documents. If a homesitter breaks the rules nobody will ask the employer for a homesitter again.

e) The term comes from the sheep themselves as sheep are usually white and a sheep with black fleece is rather an unusual exception. The black sheep in a family doesn't like work, is a sort of outsider, in some cases even a person who doesn't lead a normal life and in some cases a wrongdoer.

f) There are many ways. The best way is starting a conversation but don't ask her or him for a date immediately. It's no good being a quick worker. You can get to know people in a club, at a dancing party, during a lot of spare time activities. Don't be shy, try to be original, funny, witty and amusing, but play the part as if you aren't interested in the other person at all.

g) Yes, there are, but usually someone isn't willing to inform you about his tricks. Don't ask: "Didn't I see you on television yesterday?" It's rather silly. Play your part self-confidently, seem to be cool. I think everybody likes witty people. Don't behave awkwardly.

h) I think some of them didn't have to get to know each other as their parents or relatives arranged the match. Many got to know each other at grand balls and fairs, especially church fairs and other public merry-makings. Some got to know each other indirectly, i. e. through the help of friends. It is simpler now as the younger generation is educated together at school, young people are laxer in their manners, not so formally stiff.

i) He must be a genuine gentleman, very polite and amusing, a real master of conversation and able to behave correctly even in the finest restaurants. It's really no job for a so-called womanizer.

j) Yes, indeed it is. The lady who has hired a companion must be absolutely sure that there is no romance. It's only an agreement: You are paid for the escort, that's all.

II. Translation

1. Up to now there has been not only specialisation and this or that new service, but society has changed as well.

   Hinweis: *up to now* verlangt sinngemäß *present perfect*

2. The world/the globe has become smaller, there are big minorities. A lot of people leave their home country and immigrate, in the hope of living/leading a better and more liberal life.

   Hinweis: sinngemäß "bis jetzt", somit *has become*; *in the hope of* + *-ing*; vgl. auch *there are many ways of* + *-ing*, *opportunity of* + *-ing*, *chances* of + *-ing*; dreisilbiges *liberal* gesteigert + *more*

3. The basic rights such as freedom of speech, of assembly, of religion etc. aren't respected everywhere in the world.

   Hinweis: "sie werden geachtet" ist Passiv Gegenwart; *they will be respected* ist Zukunft

4. The social problems are even made worse by the high rate of unemployment, especially by the unemployment of young people as well. A lot of people also have difficulties in finding a flat.

   Hinweis: die Phrase *difficulty in* + *-ing*, also Hauptwort + Verhältniswort + *-ing*, auch *to be in danger of* + *-ing*, *in the hope of* + *-ing*; Er kam in der Hoffnung, eine Wohnung zu bekommen. *He came in the hope of getting a flat.*

5. In Germany the number of homeless is increasing more and more, too.

   Hinweis: immer mit doppelter Steigerung, je nach Silbenzahl; immer netter, *nicer and nicer*

6. Because of the increasing crime rate a lot of people are forced/compelled/obliged to/have to have the house guarded during the holidays or to hire a so-called housesitter.

   Hinweis: Die Phrasen für "gezwungen sein" haben natürlich eine unterschiedliche Intensität, *to have to* geht immer; etwas durch andere tun lassen, *to have* + Objekt + Mittelwort der Verg.. Er lässt das Mädchen abholen. *He has the girl collected.*

7. The reason/cause for ladies to go out with a city companion is understandable in a big city.

   Hinweis: Hauptwort + *for* + Objekt + Infinitiv *to;* siehe auch: Hier ist ein Buch, das wir lesen (sollen). *Here is a book for us to read.*

8. "I want you to accompany me. If you haven't got any time, I will stay in my hotel."

   Hinweis: die Konstruktion Zeitwort + Objekt + Infinitiv *to* auch nach *allow, advise, encourage, persuade, would like, rely on.* Ich verlasse mich darauf, dass du kommst. *I rely on you to come.*

9. "Only if my lady didn't come, I would go to the Italian restaurant with you."

   Hinweis: in Satz 8 hatten wir das Muster 1 des Bedingungssatzes, *if*-Satz Gegenwart, Hauptsatz Zukunft; hier das Muster 2: *if*-Satz 1. Vergangenheit, Hauptsatz 1. Bedingungsform

10. "If you had phoned me earlier, I would have gone out with you. It would have been a pleasure in doing it."

    Hinweis: jetzt das sogenannte 3. Muster: *if*-Satz in der dritten Vergangenheit, Hauptsatz in der 2. Bedingungsform

III. Grammar

1. a) didn't pay

   b) has dealt

   c) has worked

   d) was sitting

   Hinweis: die unterbrochene Handlung in der Verlaufsform!

   e) will have earned

   Hinweis: *by*, bis zu einem Zeitpunkt der Zukunft

2. a) "I expect you to water the flowers."

   b) "Can I count on you to feed the dog and the cat?"

   c) "I don't want the homesitter/housesitter to smoke."

   d) "It wasn't tactful of him to make friends with my daughter during my absence."

   e) "But it was important for us to have a homesitter/housesitter."

   Hinweis: in allen Fällen also Objekt + Infinitiv, in zwei Fällen zusätzlich mit Verhältniswort

3. a) I object to his marrying her/to him marrying her.

   b) Of course he can't apologize for having fallen in love.

   c) I am not thinking of informing my relatives.

d) I am used to them not telling/to their not telling me anything.

e) But I could be proud of getting such a handsome son-in-law.

Hinweis: nach jedem Verhältniswort natürlich die *ing*-Form; möglich auch *proud to get* ...; das persönliche Fürwort wird vorangestellt oder das besitzanzeigende

4. a) cleverer/more clever

b) better

Hinweis: "je ... desto" mit doppelter Steigerung

c) fewer

Hinweis: *fewer* bei der Mehrzahl; vgl. *less water*

d) least

e) further

5. a) Almost everything was made by our ancestors themselves.

b) Unfortunately, ladies are sometimes harassed.

c) Can she be protected by the companion?

d) Since 1990, single ladies have been accompanied by me.

e) A companion should be hired.

6. a) She made him call five times, but he didn't want that.

Hinweis: eher ein Zwang, also *to make* + Infinitiv ohne *to*

b) He kept the lady waiting./He made the lady wait.

c) She left her handbag in the restaurant.

Hinweis: zurücklassen, *to leave*

d) Please, let me ask questions.

Hinweis: Hier wird eine Bitte geäußert.

e) "Where do you have your hair cut?"

Hinweis: Diese "umgestellte" 2. Vergangenheit drückt aus, dass man etwas von anderen tun lässt. *have* + Objekt + Mittelwort der Vergangenheit. Ich ließ mir die Haare färben. *I had my hair dyed.*

7. a) The companion continued asking where she lived/I lived.

   Hinweis: Fragewort bleibt natürlich, aus Gegenwart wird 1. Vergangenheit, die Frageumschreibung entfällt.

   b) The companion continued asking if/whether she had to work hard/ was forced/obliged/compelled to work hard.

   Hinweis: zwei Vorgänge, a) Ersatzform von *must*, b) Verschiebung

   c) The companion continued asking how long she had been married.

   Hinweis: Fragewort bleibt, 2. Vergangenheit in die 3. Vergangenheit

   d) The companion continued asking if she liked modern music.

   e) The companion continued asking if she had attended the concert the day before.

   Hinweis: *if she attended* inzwischen auch korrekt; zu der Angabenänderung: am Tag x als Zeitangabe *yesterday;* am Tag x + 1 stimmt natürlich *yesterday* nicht mehr. Wird aber noch am gleichen Tag berichtet, bleibt *yesterday* stehen

8. a) wouldn't have met

   b) may

   Hinweis: *if*-Satz Gegenwart, Hauptsatz Hilfszeitwort auch Gegenwart; entsprechend auch *can, must*

   c) might

   Hinweis: *if*-Satz 1. Vergangenheit, Hauptsatz Vergangenheitsform *might* bleibt; entsprechend auch *should, could*

   d) couldn't have got

   Hinweis: entsprechend auch *might have got, should have got*

   e) would have been forced/compelled/obliged to/would have had to

   Hinweis: drittes Muster, Hauptsatz 2. Bedingungsform

The Tax Office

I. Questions on the text

1. a) The job of the estate agent is no male domain. Every lady can be an estate agent as well.

   b) She was a hunter.

   c) The dog was clever and obedient.

   d) Houndy could look so true-heartedly.

   e) It was no real present of a genuine animal-lover, it was only a simple malicious trick to take the dog's mind off the narcotic syringe.

   f) She was astonished at the silence. Houndy didn't bark as he usually did.

   g) The safe is normally locked by big bolts. The gangsters didn't know the code to open it.

   h) The agent had taken out an insurance policy.

   i) There was an insurance against theft, burglary and robbery. It was burglary, as the safe had been locked.

   j) She had to pay a high percentage of the money to the tax-office as the tax inspector had heard about the incident.

2. a) An estate agent organises the sale or the acquisition of houses, properties such as pieces of land, even factories or companies. There are house-agents (who buy or sell houses for or to other people only), shipping agents, travel agents.

   b) As he must find out rather soon who is willing to sell a house and find people who might buy it. Being alert is vital in this business as other agents might outdo our agent. It is always practical to know lots of people so that you are well-informed.

   c) Narcotic injections are given when you are seriously injured and suffer a lot of severe pain, or when you are operated on in a hospital.

   d) The windows are broken and there are pieces of glass everywhere. The window frame is damaged. There are scratches and dents.

e) You can insure yourself not only against theft, robbery and burglary, but also against illness, accidents, barrister's or solicitor's fees, fire and floods.

f) As I am not a lawyer I have got problems answering the question. If the dog is legally a person it was robbery, but the dog wasn't robbed. Was it robbed as a representative of our agent then? Or was it simply a thing like a safe? I think it was burglary.

g) The dog was a victim. It was injured, legally speaking, as it was drugged. You are a victim if you are killed or injured by a murderer. You can be killed in a car accident. There are victims of a war or of disease or illness. Cattle are the victims of the mad-cow-disease.

h) I must lock my car so that it's more difficult to steal it or take away things out of it. I ought to lock my house to keep out gangsters, burglars and thieves or swindlers.

i) In a tax return you must fill in some forms where you declare your income for the tax office.

j) The tax-payer had to pay a sum of money as she had tried intentionally to evade paying taxes. She had to pay a fine as a penalty for the offence.

3. a) Job is the general employment you are paid for. Usually you must enter your occupation in forms, it needn't necessarily be a job. A self-employed person has got an occupation, too. You are simply occupied in doing something, either employed or self-employed or retired. A profession needs special training at special schools or the university.

b) I need bigger offices and a lot of employees as a physician, or as a specialist of special diseases, as a manufacturer, a manager of a firm, an editor of a magazine.

c) I think it's somebody, mainly a lady, who thinks continually of better rights for the female sex and opposes male chauvinism. She doesn't like machos at all or she thinks there are machos everywhere.

d) A widow is a woman whose husband has died. She is confronted with many problems, like spending her spare time without her partner, suffering from loneliness, not having enough money, difficulties in dealing with authorities (if she didn't learn about it when her husband was still living). She usually lives on a widow's pension.

e) The list of crimes: Murder, kidnapping, rape, manslaughter, cruelty to children, blackmail, robbery, theft, burglary.

f) I would store documents, jewellery, my last will (don't throw away the key, so that the heirs and heiresses can open the safe).

g) Taxes: The value-added-tax (V.A.T.), income tax, property tax, death duties, petrol tax, motor vehicle tax, business tax, purchase tax, entertainment or admission tax, insurance taxes and a lot of indirect taxation.

h) Filling in the tax return is such a difficult thing nobody can understand how to do it. Therefore some tax-payers go to an expert. Or the tax-payers don't have time to do it, or they simply hope they don't have to pay so much tax.

i) Direct taxation: A part of your monthly wages or of your salary, a fixed percentage, is kept back for the tax-office; a self-employed person must pay the rate as well. Indirect taxation: If you pay for an article or a service you pay some percentage as indirect tax, e. g. the V.A.T. (see g above); the salt-tax is an indirect tax as well.

j) They are, indeed. The state needs money for building roads, hospitals, for the civil service, the police, the armed forces, in some cases for the unemployed, for social security and social welfare.

II. Translation

1. The estate agent needn't graduate after long university studies, he only needs a computer and a telephone.

   Hinweis: Eine häufige Fehlerquelle ist *needn't = isn't forced to, not compelled to, not obliged to, doesn't have to*; *needn't* und *doesn't have to* sind die "schwächsten" Phrasen; beachte, dass *must not = not allowed to = not permitted to*, nicht dürfen!

2. Of course he must behave extremely well and he must succeed in selling a lot.

   Hinweis: Wie gut muss das Benehmen sein, *extremely, well* ... die Umstandsangabe von *good;* Nach dem Verhältniswort steht *-ing*; neben *succeed in;* auch: *He insists on selling, I object to buying, it protects you from selling ...*

3. Before you think of selling the house, have an ad printed in the newspaper. That's cheaper than the fees for the estate agent.

   Hinweis: Den Nebensatz der Zeit kann man verkürzen: *Before thinking;* etwas durch andere tun lassen: *have* + Objekt + Mittelwort der Vergangenheit: *have an ad* ...; das einsilbige *cheap,* Steigerung *cheaper, cheapest*

4. Certainly you must spend a lot of time showing the probable buyers the house which you want to sell.

   Hinweis: *-ly* weil Umstandsangabe; der Beifügesatz nach *house:* auch *that you want to sell,* oder noch kürzer *you want to sell*

5. As soon as you see someone is interested you should draw up a contract (by the way there are forms).

   Hinweis: *should* hat Gegenwartsbedeutung

6. You can't hinder the man from leaving, you can't go to a court or ask a lawyer. Even the supreme court can't help.

   Hinweis: Verhältniswort + *-ing*: *hinder from leaving*; anstatt *can't = aren't able to*

7. But you will need the help of a lawyer, if the tax inspector comes and checks all the accounts.

   Hinweis: Hier liegt ein Bedingungssatz, 1. Muster vor: *if*-Satz Gegenwart, Hauptsatz Zukunft.

8. The tax must be paid, even if you are against it and are tired of paying. Nobody likes to pay taxes.

   Hinweis: *must be paid,* Leideform + Hilfszeitwort, z. B. auch *can be paid, should be paid, ought to be paid, may be paid, might be paid,* kann, sollte, sollte, darf, dürfte bezahlt werden; auch *against paying* ist möglich, *-ing* nach dem Verhältniswort: *tired of paying;* siehe auch *I am fond of paying,* ich zahle gern, *I am used to paying,* ich bin ans Zahlen gewöhnt; *to* ist hier kein Infinitiv-*to,* sondern ein Verhältniswort; nach *like* kann auch *-ing* stehen, *Nobody likes paying taxes.*

9. The state insists on our doing it and you can't excuse yourself for having forgotten it.

   Hinweis: *insist on + -ing,* Verhältniswort + *-ing;* anstatt *our doing* kann auch *us doing* stehen; *for + -ing* gleichfalls, in diesem Fall als Vergangenheitsform *having* + Mittelwort der Verg.

10. You can't simply solve the problem by emigrating into a tax haven, apart from your wife opposing it.
    Hinweis: Natürlich wieder *by + -ing,* Verhältniswort + *-ing;* entsprechend *from + -ing;* anstelle von *wife* kann auch *wife's* stehen

III. Grammar

1. a) Must you lock the safe?/Do you have to lock the safe?/Are you obliged to lock the safe?/Are you compelled to lock the safe?

   b) Must I buy .../Do I have to buy .../Am I obliged to buy .../Am I compelled to buy a better safe?
   Hinweis: *Am I forced to* auch möglich; *needn't*, nicht müssen!

   c) Did you have to take out an insurance policy?
   Hinweis: andere Formen nicht sinnvoll

   d) May I dodge the tax?/Am I allowed to dodge the tax?/Am I permitted to dodge the tax?
   Hinweis: *mustn't*, nicht dürfen!

   e) Were you at the meeting?

2. a) systematically
   Hinweis: auf *-ic* + *-al*

   b) enthusiastically

   c) simply

   d) completely true-heartedly
   Hinweis: Wie schaute er drein?, nicht: Wie schaute er aus?

   e) extraordinarily good
   Hinweis: nach *taste* nicht *well;* Vgl. *He sings well.*

3. a) of opening/to open

   b) of going hunting/to go hunting

   c) to hunt

   d) in chasing/chasing

   e) of killing

4. a) After hearing/Having heard/After having heard its master, the dog begins to bark.

   b) After leaving/After having left/Having left the house, she went to a hunters' assembly.

   c) Before entering the house, she shouted "Houndy!"

   d) There was a tax inspector checking the receipts.

   e) Not filling in the forms correctly, she was fined.

5. a) She has had the safe repaired.

   b) The burglary was her worst experience.

   c) "What shall I do?"/"What am I to do?"/"What am I expected/supposed/told to do?"
   Hinweis: *shall* nur mit *I* und *we* bei Frage und Gegenwart!

   d) "I should/ought to telephone the insurance company now."

   e) "I couldn't come home earlier."/"I wasn't able to come home earlier."

6. a) hadn't read

   b) we must/we will have to

   c) wouldn't do

   d) heard

   e) wouldn't have been

7. a) on getting/to get

   b) of living/to live

   c) in the chairman's killing/in the chairman killing

   d) of your asking/of you asking

   e) from having

How to Find Time for Thinking

I. Questions on the text

1. a) The artillery is the part of the army where your tympanic membranes can be injured. It's because of the loud bang.

   b) They learn about it so as to prevent injuries.

   c) Both the recruit and the pupil must obey.

   d) Discipline is vital for learning and thinking.

   e) He simply didn't hear what the maths teacher was teaching.

   f) We get lots of information daily, thousands of items are poured over us daily.

   g) He simply must watch TV or work with the internet, he can't free himself from it by himself.

   h) They are not TV stars or entertainers or actors or actresses.

   i) It is unfortunate if you don't listen to somebody in cases when accidents are possible.

   j) He was simply interested whether the pupil was able to listen and to concentrate.

2. a) People hold their hands over their ears when there is a big noise, or when there are explosions.

   b) It's a principle that pupils and grown-ups forget things heard only once very soon.

   c) I must use a ruler and a pair of compasses. I must use a pencil or a ballpoint pen of course for drawing.

   d) The quadrature of the circle would solve the problem of the length round the outside of a circle simply by construction. The existing formula for calculating the length isn't exact, only an approximation.

   e) Mr Ritemayor would become a famous man and maybe he would be given the Nobel Prize.

   f) He was rather angry.

g) A superfluous question is a question that isn't necessary. I can ask a man who is just drinking a glass of beer in a pub: "Do you like beer?"

h) In the open air a shelter is a sort of small building which protects you from rain and wind or a storm.

i) It's a job of great responsibility. If a nurse isn't attentive dangerous consequences might arise.

j) If she had known about it she would have reacted in a way which might have influenced the result in the intended way.

3. a) That is a "beginner" in the armed forces or a soldier in the first year.

b) Ranks: the general, the admiral, air commander, colonel general, major-general, lieutenant-general, general-staff officer, major, lieutenant, colonel, sergeant, corporal.

c) The soldiers live and sleep in the barracks. All the buildings together are the barracks. Are there barracks in your home town?

d) Everybody was roaring with laughter when the teacher entered the classroom, wearing two different shoes. Or: I can't forget a teacher of mine at the grammar school who wore brown and black shoes simultaneously.

e) An entirely polite fellow is somebody who greets everybody all the time, or says hello to you ten times a day, or takes off his hat, or offers you your seat in the Underground.

f) Young folk, pay attention. These denim jeans FASHIONABLE make you irresistible. Buy them right now. Don't wait until somebody else buys them and puts you in the shade.

g) It's not the real world. It's the world invented by the computer on the monitor.

h) We must persuade them to visit psychologists or specialists who can help, we must persuade them to stay in special hospitals with special treatment.

i) They must put on elegant suits or clothes and think of the answers they will have to give to any questions.

j) Why do you want to be a ...? What are your hobbies? What are your favourite subjects at school? Can you work in a group? Do you smoke? Are you a member of a club?

II. Translation

1. You must admit that the general is more experienced than the recruit and therefore you must obey him.

   Hinweis: *must* ist natürlich austauschbar durch *you have to admit;* die anderen Ersatzformen sind intensiver, etwa *you are forced to/compelled to/obliged to admit,* sie passen eher im zweiten Fall: *you are forced to obey*

2. If a rooky has less money, he needn't necessarily have fewer friends (or girl-friends).

   Hinweis: *less* vor einem Einzahlwort, *fewer* vor einem Mehrzahlwort

3. The higher the rank, the fewer friends someone has or just those who expect some advantages.

   Hinweis: je – desto, *the – the* + Steigerung; der notwendige Nebensatz auch in anderer Form: *those that ..., those expecting ...*

4. Discipline in the army is as necessary as at school, or do you possibly believe it isn't necessary at school?

   Hinweis: beim Vergleich so ... wie, *as ... as;* bei Verneinung neben *isn't as necessary* auch *isn't so necessary; possibly* ist bei der Frage vorzuziehen, ansonst *might*

5. I am afraid many pupils, especially girls, think: "The younger a teacher is, the better, the older, the worse." But are the older ones more considerate or more understanding? Has anyone got any further questions?

   Hinweis: *the ... the* + Steigerung, je ... desto; einsilbiges Eigenschaftswort, Steigerung *-er;* dreisilbiges *more;* zweisilbiges Eigenschaftswort: wenn die Endung nicht auf *-er, le* nach Mitlaut, *-y, ow,* dann *more; ones* ist das Ersatzwort für das Hauptwort Lehrer; *further* wird hier bevorzugt, bei Entfernungen eher *farther*

6. Even the most beautiful, the youngest, the most elegant, the most charming one wants you to learn something and to get any qualifications.

   Hinweis: der Superlativ: einsilbiges Eigenschaftswort: *-est;* zweisilbig entsprechend oben Kommentar 5, *-est* oder *most;* dreisilbig *-most; want* + Objekt + Infinitiv *-to*

7. Do pupils want the teacher to wear the latest fashion? Is it essential? An anonymous poll in the classroom showed that a tie is generally rejected.

   Hinweis: zu *want* siehe Kommentar zu 6; *latest* hat den Sinn von neuest; vgl. dazu *last,* letzte(r), letztes; *is rejected;* Leideform, Gegenwart

8. Sandra, with whom I always play tennis, hates ties and suits, she thinks only denim jeans which are imported from the USA are fashionable.

   Hinweis: Unterscheide nicht-notwendige und notwendige Beifügesätze! Im ersten Fall gibt es nur diese eine Form Komma + *with whom ...*; im zweiten Fall ist der Nebensatz notwendig, also mehrere Möglichkeiten: *that are imported/imported ...*

9. Monica, whose dad owns a fashion shop, only likes suits which are made in Italy.

   Hinweis: *whose* männlich, weiblich und sächlich, nicht notwendiger Nebensatz, mit Komma; der notwendige Nebensatz *which are made/that are made/made in ...* ohne Komma

10. Do you know the two blondes in the jeans shop, Cissy and Mary, one of whom is a tailoress? I know a girl who wears elegant silk blouses and black skirts.

    Hinweis: Der erste Nebensatz ist eine nicht notwendige Information. Hier kann man nichts austauschen oder verändern. Der zweite Nebensatz ist notwendig, somit auch *that wears ...* oder einfach *wearing ...*; entsprechend auch beim Passivsinn: *Do you know the girls who are invited .../that are invited ...* oder "verkürzt" *the girls invited ...*; sächlich: *which* bzw. *that* bzw. "verkürzt": *The book which sells best .../that sells .../selling ...; The books which are imported .../that are imported .../imported.*

III. Grammar

1. a) The teacher told us (them)/had told us/would tell us to pay attention.

   Hinweis: bei Befehlen *say* durch *tell* "austauschen"

   b) The teacher said (that) in his lessons there was no chaos.

   c) The teacher said (that) they had to draw a circle then.

   Hinweis: andere Ersatzformen wenig sinnvoll

   d) The teacher said (that) he couldn't/wasn't able to solve the problem of the quadrature of the circle.

   e) The teacher said (that) we (they) should give up.

   Hinweis: *should, could, might, ought to* wird unverändert übernommen

2. a) most skilful

   b) least

   c) more quickly / faster

   Hinweis: bei Umstandsangaben immer mit *more* steigern, außer bei Ausnahmen, die auch im Positiv kein *-ly* haben, z. B. *fast, hard*

d) more / better
Hinweis: je – desto

e) best / less / fewer

3. a) The quadrature of the circle is as difficult as the production of petrol out of water.

b) The maths teacher wears the latest suits.

c) He lives far away, but not so far as Mr Heetsy, who has to go a longer distance (by car).

d) Yesterday I met a teacher who goes by train for 2 ½ hours daily.
Hinweis: oder die Verkürzung des Beifügesatzes: *teacher going by ...*

e) He lives in a house which was built in the late 19th century.
Hinweis: Verkürzung: *house built in ...*

f) The information is no longer noticed./These pieces of information are no longer noticed.
Hinweis: *pieces of information* wird selten verwendet; *information* ist Mehrzahl.

g) In the computer the real world is imitated.

h) For decades scientists have occupied themselves with the "calculator".

i) For some time the computer has been used in the classrooms.

j) Optimists forecast that in the year 2000 a computer will be used in every household.

4. a) Does he like maths?

b) Must he attend/Does he have to attend/Is he obliged to attend special courses?

c) May he/Is he allowed to/Is he permitted to give up his plans?

d) Has he studied the problem?/For how long has he studied the problem?

e) Will he succeed?

How to Become More Interesting

I. Questions on the text

1. a) They either retreat into their rooms or they leave the house.

   b) They think the garments they wear suit them.

   c) Dad is more understanding as he thinks his daughter is growing up and no longer a child.

   d) The trousers or blouses which were found in the attic demonstrate that they were in many years ago.

   e) Piercing is shocking.

   f) The young girl was trying to pierce herself.

   g) They say only bulls have nose-rings.

   h) Yes, they can. Before long the new habit will be old-fashioned.

   i) No, they can't. Even the strictest parents can't prevent their children from doing something.

   j) You and your parents should try to solve the problems together.

2. a) There are many ways of becoming more interesting: You can drive a flashy car or motor-bike, you can try to be the best in an event, to play the piano excellently, drink a cup of coffee with a film star in the café.

   b) "You really shouldn't listen to this awful music." "You must not stay out until midnight." "You can't go out on Christmas Day."

   c) I lay sulkily on my couch one day because my parents didn't allow me to visit my friend.

   d) I was extremely angry and very furious and rather aggressive.

   e) They are necessary for your personal development because you must learn to become independent and say what you think.

   f) "Oh, it's really shocking. She is so bad at school and spends most of her time in discos." "Her parents aren't wealthy at all, but the daughters wear clothes in the latest style."

g) I turn my nose up at people who have got quite different habits or do striking things.

h) A bull is very strong. You can only lead it when it has got a nose-ring. It's very painful for it when you hold it by the ring and it wants to run away.

i) Of course. You can wear shoes with very high heels, overalls with braces, you can carry a rucksack instead of a bag, you can wear loose fitting trousers.

j) They must educate me. Without them I am rather helpless. I can grow up only with my parents.

3. a) I think it is. Many famous and well-known pop stars, singers, film-stars and sportsmen are the heroes for young people as they want to be as good and famous as they are.

b) I think they can depend on commercials as the spots influence us and suggest to us that we are modern people if we buy or eat this or that. If a star or showman advertises for something, you are at least as good as him if you buy it.

c) Heroes are people who are famous and well-known, especially pop singers or sportsmen. Usually young people wear the same clothes. See question 3 a above.

d) I think in some cases it's true as many people tend to believe people who wear elegant suits or dresses more than others who prefer casual wear or even unusual clothing.

e) I can. Special clothing is appropriate at a wedding ceremony or party, at any solemn ceremony, at any formal parties. I think worn jeans aren't appropriate when you attend a religious service or a funeral.

f) I am absolutely convinced that sexy clothing is no good. There are better ways of drawing the attention of other people or the other sex.

g) I am allowed to dress up at a fancy dress party or at the carnival. People do so as they want to have fun and play a different role (their "hidden" desire).

h) A suit or costume off the peg is much cheaper and there is a bigger choice. Of course you must try on many outfits in order to see whether one fits. The tailor takes his measuring tape and measures you. The suit fits excellently. If you aren't slim go to the tailor, but it will be rather expensive.

i) You wear a formal dress at formal parties, e. g. a suit or an evening-dress, an elegant costume (See question 3 e above); you can wear casual wear or clothes in your spare time. You can wear that sort outdoors. Casual wear is rather comfortable.

j) The industry is interested in frequent changes as it wants to get more money by selling new clothing. Younger people are the better customers as they want to wear the latest fashion. As a girl of 16 you can't wear the same as you wore when you were seven.

II. Translation

1. Before the girl lay down angrily on the couch she locked the door.

   Hinweis: Der Zeitnebensatz kann verkürzt werden: *Before lying down ... the girl locked ...* In diesem Fall muss im Hauptsatz *girl* nochmals erscheinen, weil es sonst "verloren geht".

2. While she was reading a magazine which she had just bought the day before, she was listening to the radio.

   Hinweis: Das Bindewort *while* verlangt sinngemäß die Verlaufsform; auch hier die Verkürzung *while reading...*; der (notwendige) Beifügesatz kann auch heißen: *that she .../magazine she had bought.*

3. After she had read an extraordinarily interesting article and had calmed down she discussed it with her mother.

   Hinweis: Auch hier ist die Verkürzung des Zeitnebensatzes möglich: *After having read/ Having read/After reading ...*; oder auch: *After having calmed down/Having calmed.../ After calming ...*

4. Usually she calms down after she has read something interesting.

   Hinweis: der Zeitnebensatz verkürzt: *After having read/Having read/After reading; read* ist hier natürlich die dritte Form: *read, read, read*

5. The old silk blouses which she found in the attic had once belonged to her aunt.

   Hinweis: der Beifügesatz auch: *blouses that she .../blouses she found ...*

6. The friend who wears torn denim jeans has (at least in my view) the strictest parents, but they can't stop her from wearing these jeans.
   Hinweis: der Beifügesatz auch: *friend that wears .../friend wearing ...*; Superlativ einsilbig *-est; -ing* nach einem Verhältniswort: *from wearing ...*

7. The denim jeans which are sold in the supermarket aren't as chic as those from the up-to-date boutique, are they?
   Hinweis: Der Passiv-Beifügesatz kann ebenfalls verkürzt werden: *jeans sold in the ...*; unabhängig davon kann *which* auch durch *that* ausgetauscht werden; beim verneinten Vergleich kann anstatt *as* auch *so* stehen: *aren't so chic.*

8. After she had been told to buy new clothing, she went to Munich by car with her friend.
   Hinweis: Passivzeitnebensatz: auch *After being told ... /After having been told ...*

9. After they had done their shopping, they went into the ice-cream parlour and ordered some ice-cream.
   Hinweis: auch *After having done ... /After doing ... /Having done ...*

10. After they had come home, they drank some cups of coffee before they unpacked their clothes.
    Hinweis: auch möglich: *After coming home ... /Having come home ... /After having come home ...*; beachte auch *they had come,* sie waren ...; die Veränderungen und Verkürzungen sind nur bei notwendigen Beifügesätzen möglich; bei nicht-notwendigen Einschüben gibt es nur die eine Form (siehe oben); Verkürzungen auch beim Zeitnebensatz und beim Grundnebensatz (siehe dort)

III. Grammar

1. a) As/because she didn't like ordinary trousers, she wore tight black jeans.

   b) The person over there who is wearing high heels is her cousin.
   Hinweis: Verlaufsform sinngemäß notwendig

   c) After she had been lying/After she was lying/After she had lain on the couch, she went shopping.

   d) Before she tried the things on she was in 20 shops at least.

   e) Because her mum doesn't like mini skirts she always starts arguing about them.

2. a) Shouted at for wearing these jeans I was lying sulkily on the couch.

   b) Seeing my pierced navel she was shocked.

   c) The blouses bought in Paris are over there.

   d) After having her lips pierced/Having her lips pierced/After piercing her lips she went to the café.

   e) The jeans are displayed in the shop window before being sold.

3. a) She had her ears pierced.

   b) I object to you/your wearing this black underwear.

   c) You shouldn't tear your jeans intentionally.

   d) You are making a mistake if you think that's terrific.

   e) I wonder why you refuse to do it. You are burdening yourself.
   Hinweis: "solltest" (c) Gegenwart, aber "sich irren" (d) ohne rückbezügliches Fürwort, wie auch "sich fragen", "sich weigern"; aber "sich belasten", *to burden oneself*

4. a) We all are used to wearing these clothes.
   Hinweis: *to* hier Verhältniswort, kein Infinitiv-*to*

   b) These jeans/this pair of jeans is/are good for wearing in your spare time.

   c) You shouldn't buy them without trying them on.

   d) Instead of complaining you should choose some other ones.

   e) I have pleasure in possessing a lot of jeans.
   Hinweis: Bei keinem Satz ist der Infinitiv möglich.

5. a) Do you know the girl whose parents are jeans manufacturers?

   b) Cissy Cranford, who is 22 years old, is a friend of mine.
   Hinweis: nicht-notwendiger Einschub, 2-mal Komma, *that* nicht möglich

   c) This jewel ring, which cost GBP 5,000, belongs to my mum.
   Hinweis: wie in b

d) The girl with whom/who I went shopping with/that I went shopping with/girl I went shopping with hates piercing.

Hinweis: notwendiger Nebensatz: Welches Mädchen? Verschiedene Möglichkeiten sind bereits bekannt.

e) Superstar ist the most elegant shop which you can find/that you can find/shop you can find.

Hinweis: notwendige Ergänzung

6. a) ... are they?

b) ... can't it?

c) ... don't we?

d) ... won't we?

e) ... will we?

Hinweis: positive Aussage, negatives "Anhängsel", *question tag,* und umgekehrt. Beim "Vollverb" im Gegensatz zum Hilfszeitwort *don't,* bzw. *didn't*. Alle anderen Zeitstufen sind ohnehin zusammengesetzt, z. B. *we have, ... havent't we*.

The Grand Ball

I. Questions on the text

1. a) It was a rather striking poster. It was the lady who might have drawn his attention.

   b) There was a longer stop at the railway station, he had to wait for the connection.

   c) He was used to watching something for some time before he started.

   d) They kissed enthusiastically and gently and tenderly.

   e) He didn't want to miss his connection, he glanced secretly so that the girl couldn't see it. She might have thought the boy wasn't paying his full attention to her.

   f) She would have become very angry because she would have thought he behaved extremely badly.

   g) I think she thought the boy didn't like her any more or wasn't interested in her any longer.

   h) Nobody could see then where the letter came from, e. g. the girl's mum or dad or her sisters and brothers.

   i) I think he was amused as the letter had come back in a rather unusual way and all the mysterious ways had been in vain; the boy blushed as everything was discovered.

   j) Do you understand the sudden reactions of girls? I don't. She may have given him the wrong address as she was disappointed that he left hastily or she was even annoyed.

2. a) He must leave a train or bus if this train goes to a town or destination he doesn't want to go to and he gets on another train then.

   b) I think the fire brigade got money from the members of the brigade or the drinks cost more than usual.

   c) There were dancers of every age, from youngsters to grown-ups and pensioners and they had different tastes in music.

d) I don't know. It might be the same girl like in the text. I like girls with brunette or black hair. I prefer girls with long hair. I don't like curls. I don't like over-self-confident girls.
The boy must be handsome, self-confident, strong, witty.

e) I might be in high spirits at my first date with the most wonderful girl, or when a girl says that she likes me or when I have won in the lottery.

f) Hello, it was one of the nicest evenings I ever spent. You are so fascinating and the best-looking girl in the world. I can't forget you ...

g) I usually blush when there is an embarrassing situation or when there is a mishap I feel ashamed of.

h) A grand ball is a formal event where you must wear formal clothing and everything is a bit solemn. Disco dancing isn't so stiff and you can relax.

i) They simply telephone or fax somebody.

j) He or she must be reliable and faithful, humorous, helpful, tender, self-confident.

3. a) The fire brigade or the firemen or fire fighters must fight fires, i. e. put out fires. In some cases they help in emergencies and accidents and rescue people or clear up roads after an accident.

b) I can join the brigade or pay monthly subscriptions or I can make a special donation to the brigade.

c) They are put up on big notice boards or advertising columns. You shouldn't put them up on walls, fences or trees or the walls of bus shelters.

d) You meet a person at a particular time. A blind date is a rendezvous where you have never seen the girl or young man before, there was only a telephone call or a written notice.

e) I take a letter to the post office or put it into a post box.

f) They want to know everything and are eager to get informed about everything.

g) They feel something must be wrong or they have done some mischief.

h) They are angry when you have done something wrong or you haven't done what you were expected to do.

i) I want to be independent and free and don't want to be closed in by you.

j) They didn't have motor vehicles then. Now almost everybody has a car and there are fewer passengers on the trains. Fewer people write letters, they simply telephone or fax.

II. Translation

1. The door of the train didn't open automatically. The conductor, who was sent for immediately, was to open it.

   Hinweis: sich öffnen, *to open;* zum rückbezüglichen Fürwort *oneself,* siehe dort; der Beifügesatz ist nicht notwendig, ist ein Einschub, deshalb Komma und nur eine Form; ... er sollte ... 1. Vergangenheit, verschiedene Möglichkeiten außer *to be to: He was expected to open/he was supposed to open/he was told to* ... je nach unterlegtem Sinn: Man erwartete es, man vermutete es, es war ein Auftrag; *to be said to* passt hier nicht so gut: *He was said to* ... man sagte es von ihm, dass ...

2. Neither he nor the mechanic were able to open it, but then it opened suddenly all by itself.

   Hinweis: siehe auch *either – or,* entweder – oder; das Hilfszeitwort *can* kann ich schwerlich in die Vergangenheit "verschieben" (Ausnahme: Frage, Verneinung, Wahrnehmung); somit die Ersatzform *to be able;* Frage: *Could he?* Verneinung: *He couldn't;* Wahrnehmung: *He could see, hear* etc.; immer natürlich auch: *Was able to ...? He wasn't able to ...; itself* ist kein rückbezügliches Fürwort, sondern ein betonendes "selber", "selbst"

3. As all the passengers were good-tempered, they didn't blame the conductor for it.

   Hinweis: anstatt *as* auch *because*; der Grundnebensatz verkürzt: *Being good-tempered, the passengers didn't blame ...*

4. As our young man didn't want to stay in the waiting lounge of the station, he went to the fire brigade grand ball.

   Hinweis: Grundnebensatz verkürzt: *Not wanting to stay ... our young man went ...*

5. Did he fall in love with the girl with whom he spent the evening? Why couldn't he stay any longer? Why did he have to leave the girl?
   Hinweis: notwendiger Beifügesatz auch: ... *who he spent the evening with/... that he spent the evening with ...*; Frage: *couldn't* möglich, natürlich auch ... *wasn't he able to ...*; musste: Umschreibung ... *Did he have to?/Was he forced to?/Was he obliged to?/Was he compelled to?* Die Ersatzformen haben eine unterschiedliche Intensität.

6. (For) how long may you stay in the disco? In earlier years the girls were often only allowed to go to a grand ball, if they were invited/had been invited. Since the discos have come into existence, there have been fewer grand balls.
   Hinweis: "dürfen", Gegenwart: *may* (auch *can*), *to be allowed to;* in der Vergangenheit und Zukunft nur *to be allowed to (to be permitted to)*; Leideform: Ich werde gewöhnlich eingeladen: *I am usually invited;* ich wurde eingeladen: *I was invited;* ich werde eingeladen werden: *I will be invited*

7. "You are to be good." "Yes, we should behave ourselves at the grand ball."
   Hinweis: "sollen": *to be to, to be expected ...* (siehe oben); *should (ought to)* immer Gegenwartsbedeutung; sich benehmen + *oneself,* (auch ohne möglich)

8. Yesterday, he was to buy the tickets for the grand ball. But he had to prepare himself for the English test.
   Hinweis: "er sollte", Vergangenheit; "sich vorbereiten" + *oneself*

9. If you don't pick me up for the grand ball, I will be angry with you. Since my 17th birthday I have been picked up by you.
   Hinweis: *if* + Verneinung oder *unless you pick ... up;* Bedingungssatz Gegenwart + Zukunft; *since* + Zeitpunkt: 2. Vergangenheit, hier Leideform

10. If you had telephoned me earlier, I wouldn't have been picked up by your brother.
    Hinweis: Bedingungssatz 3. Vergangenheit + 2. Bedingungsform

III. Grammar

1. a) Was the girl angry?

   b) Was he glad about the dance?

   c) Was he interested in her?

   d) Did he enjoy himself?

   e) He didn't introduce himself.

2. a) Did he get the letter himself?
   b) The officials in the post office opened the letter themselves.
   c) "I remember the ball myself."
   d) "Yes, I fell in love, it happened by itself."
   e) The girl thinks only of herself.

3. a) They both saw each other for the first time.
   b) Did they fall in love?
   c) No, they didn't quarrel.
   d) Yes, they kissed.
   e) They looked at each other tenderly.

4. a) He says/has said/will say (that) he likes balls.
   b) He says/has said/will say (that) he prefers modern hits.
   c) He says/has said/will say (that) he must try to find her.
   d) He says/has said/will say (that) he oughn't to look for her.
   e) He says/has said/will say (that) he thinks she may not/mustn't see him.

   Hinweis: Natürlich wird die Zeit der direkten Rede nicht verändert, wenn das berichtende Zeitwort in der Gegenwart, 2. Vergangenheit, Zukunft steht!

5. a) He said/had said/would say (that) he liked balls.
   b) He said/had said/would say (that) he preferred modern hits.
   c) He said/had said/would say (that) he had to try to find her.

   Hinweis: andere Ersatzformen wenig sinnvoll

   d) He said/had said/would say (that) he oughtn't to look for her.

   Hinweis: Wie *should* wird auch *ought to* unverändert übernommen.

   e) He said/had said/would say (that) he thought she wasn't allowed to/ mightn't see him.

   Hinweis: *might* nur in der indirekten Rede als "verschobenes" *may;* ansonst *might,* dürfte, könnte, eventuell

6. a) He always asks/has asked/will ask what he is to do/he is expected to do/supposed to do/told to do.

   Hinweis: Hier muss man *shall* austauschen, da es nur in der Frage (*I, we,* Gegenwart) "sollen" bedeutet.

   b) He always asks/has asked/will ask where he should go.

   c) He always asks/has asked/will ask if/whether you/he can help him.

   d) He always asks/has asked/will ask if/whether you/he could support him.

   e) He always asks/has asked/will ask if you/he understand/understands girls.

   Hinweis: siehe oben 4 a – e

7. a) He always asked/had asked/would ask what he should/was to/was expected to/was supposed to do.

   Hinweis: nur hier in der indirekten Frage ist *should* das "verschobene" *shall;* sonst *should* nur Gegenwart, sollte (jetzt)

   b) He always asked/had asked/would ask where he should go.

   Hinweis: *should* unverändert!

   c) He always asked/had asked/would ask if/whether you/he/she could help him/were able to help him/was able to help him.

   Hinweis: nur hier *could* als verschobenes *can;* ansonsten *could,* könnte; nur im Fragesatz oder bei Verneinung und bei "sehen", "hören" usw. auch konnte; man liest aber immer häufiger *could* in positiven Sätzen

   d) He always asked/had asked/would ask if/whether you/he could support him.

   Hinweis: *could* bleibt unverändert!

   e) He always asked/had asked/would ask if/whether he/you understood girls.

   Hinweis: Bei "berichtendem" Zeitwort in der 1. Vergangenheit, 3. Vergangenheit und 1. Bedingungsform "Verschiebungen", außer *should* und *could*

8. a) to dance/dancing

   b) to attend

   c) dancing

d) giving

e) to write

Hinweis: Entsprechende Tabellen finden sich im Lehrbuch; auch das Wörterbuch gibt an, was nach einem bestimmten Zeitwort zu folgen hat. Im Übrigen wurde hier auf Zeitwort + Verhältniswort verzichtet, wo ohnehin nur die *-ing*-Form steht!

The Incident

I. Questions on the text

1. a) He didn't like ringing the bells in winter as it was already dark and he feared being alone in the church.

   b) He believed that the saints would stop such a robbery or theft or they would protect themselves.

   c) No, he didn't share his opinion. As we have a free will, no saint interferes.

   d) We had a long discussion about it.

   e) I am not satisfied, either, as I can't understand that God allows such accidents to happen, or as the boy's mother sighed: God has taken away my son. But God himself has created the law of nature.

   f) The church is a special building different from the world outside. The church is a most holy place. A lot of things are forbidden.

   g) He was unemployed and his wife didn't like him any longer.

   h) He intended to confess his sins there and not in his parish church as the parson and he knew each other very well.

   i) He didn't know that the parson was in the abbey even in the confessional. He had miscalculated.

   j) He asked him whether he had had a nice trip. He said that the weather was fine. So Uncle Charles realised that the parson was in the confessional. Otherwise he wouldn't have noticed it first.

2. a) St Michael was the patron saint of the knights as it was a duty of the knight to fight against evil. The chief angel or archangel Michael fought against evil ghosts and the devil.

   b) The bells are no longer rung by ropes you have to pull, they are rung electrically.

   c) Possibly he thought the parson or the sacristan had taken it away in order to mend it or to varnish it; or the statue had been given to a museum or an exhibition on loan.

d) A law of nature is something which happens without people who interfere. Isaac Newton discovered the laws of gravitation or: Why does the apple drop? Because of the law of inertia you fall down when there is a sudden stop in the train or bus.

e) If I am the witness of a crime, I will watch everything very closely or carefully and call the police. I know in a lot of cases I must help or rescue the victim alone or with the help of others. I only watch and phone the police if the gangster is armed or very violent. The police advise you to do so.

f) There are a lot of reasons for being desperate. I think I would be desperate if a friend of mine had died or my mum or dad, or my friend had left me or if I myself or a friend of mine was seriously ill. I can talk with friends, experienced adults, teachers, priests, psychologists. I can try to take my mind off it by doing a lot of things, e. g. by going abroad.

g) A psychologist helps you when you suffer from light or serious mental illnesses like neurosis or psychosis. He tries to understand you and solve your problems. He tries to heal diseases of the mind and in some cases diseases of the body.

h) In some cases school can be sad, too. School is not an island, it has got the same problems and sad moments. Subjectively there are the same problems as adults have.

i) He may have relaxed there, i. e. after an illness. He spent his holidays in the abbey.

j) Stealing, robbing, cheating, insulting, offending, mobbing, being unfaithful; to lie, to hate, to be aggressive, to murder, to tease, to misuse.

3. a) Handicapped children are not only a problem for the disabled themselves but also for their parents; a black sheep in the family is a burden; high debts are a burden indeed; incurable diseases or irreparable problems might be burdens.

b) It is a difficult question indeed. I think there are fewer and fewer working places, mainly because of automation. Another reason are the high wages or salary and the high rate of taxes and insurances contrary to other countries where things can be manufactured more cheaply.

c) You have got less money, and so you can buy only fewer things and the manufacturers sell fewer articles.

d) In this case they can't get everything they like from clothing, toys to sports kit and food.

e) Usually problems arise. Children are lazy (sometimes?), don't work hard, in a few cases the parents think their children are treated unfairly and they have to complain about it, or there is a reprimand because of bad behaviour.

f) That's a difficult question, indeed. First of all don't marry too hastily, i. e. go steady for a long time first. Try to solve problems and don't give up at once. Ask friends or marriage consultants for help. Avoid flirtations which might be the first step towards separating.

g) They often say they want to lead a trial marriage in order to find out if they are good partners; or they think they can avoid the problems and costs of a divorce; or they can simply part when they don't like each other any more.

h) There are many disadvantages. The children often suffer if they have no "real" parents; problems arise when the romance ends and how to share the furniture, the house, the car. There is no solicitor who helps you.

i) There are a lot of consequences. Usually one partner is rather disappointed. Normally one partner must provide for the partner who left him or her; in some cases the property is lost, e. g. a house; the children suffer under the separation of their parents.

j) Not everything is perfect. Today's problems will be solved tomorrow and won't be a burden any more. I think my burdens are light. There are lots of people especially in the Third or Fourth World who have got more serious problems such as hunger or incurable diseases. Unemployment and crimes and contagious diseases, e.g. the human immunodeficiency virus, HIV, are serious problems.

II. Translation

1. The sacristan said (that) St Michael was the patron saint of the parish church.

   Hinweis: In der wörtlichen Rede würde es heißen: *"St Michael is the patron saint."* Ist das sogenannte berichtende Zeitwort der nicht-wörtlichen, indirekten Rede in der Gegenwart, dann ändert sich nichts: *The sacristan (always) says (that) St Michael is the* ... Wenn das berichtende Zeitwort in der Vergangenheit steht, wird auch *is* zu *was* "verschoben": ... *said* ... *St Michael was* ... Siehe dazu auch III.

2. Are the church bells rung by the server or the sacristan? They have been rung both by the sacristan and the server for a decade.

   Hinweis: Beachte die Leideform, das Passiv in der Gegenwart! Vergleiche dazu: Die Glocken werden geläutet werden. *The bells will be rung.* "Seit" signalisiert 2. Vergangenheit, *present perfect.*

3. The parson instructed us about free will intensively. We discussed the problem for a long time, indeed. Since that lesson we have occupied ourselves with that./Since that lesson we have been occupying ourselves with that.

   Hinweis: *ourselves* ist das rückbezügliche Fürwort, *reflexive pronoun.* Manchmal muß man es nehmen, manchmal nicht, siehe auch folgende Aufgaben! Im Wörterbuch steht im ersteren Fall *oneself* bzw. *o. s.*

4. The sermon was interrupted, believe me. The man couldn't control himself.

   Hinweis: "sich beherrschen", *to control oneself*

5. He refused to leave the church and to apologize.

   Hinweis: *refuse* und *apologize* bleiben ohne *oneself,* obwohl "sich".

6. The parson was angry and even afraid of the man. "The man doesn't behave", people said.

   Hinweis: auch *to be angry* und *to be afraid* ohne reflexive, genau so wie *to behave,* (auch mit *oneself* möglich)

7. Do you remember the accident? Do you still know, when the incident happened?
   Hinweis: *remember* und *happen* ohne *oneself*

8. At first they fell in love, then they quarrelled and parted.
   Hinweis: das sogenannte "wechselbezügliche" Fürwort, *reciprocal pronoun* nicht bei *to fall in love, to quarrel, to part*; vergleiche dazu: Sie sehen sich, einander. *They see each other.*

9. They haven't seen each other again, they don't get along with each other any more.
   Hinweis: zweimal das *reciprocal pronoun*

10. Has it happened by itself/all by itself? He hasn't found a solution (by) himself.
    Hinweis: Das sogenannte betonende Fürwort, *emphasizing pronoun* hat die Bedeutung "selber", "selbst". Dieses Fürwort geht auch dann, wenn das reflexive "verboten" ist: Ich erinnere mich: *I remember.* Ich erinnere mich schon selber: *I remember myself.*

III. Grammar

1. a) The man said that he had been full of despair.
   Hinweis: Neben der dritten Vergangenheit kann auch die vorliegende 1. stehenbleiben: *that he was ...*

   b) The man said that his wife would leave him.

   c) The man said that by the following Sunday she would have left him.

   d) The man said that in earlier times she had never been unfaithful.

   e) The man said that she would move out of their flat the following day/the day after and that he didn't understand all those things.
   Hinweis: Die Veränderungen der Zeitangabe, des besitzanzeigendes Fürworts und der Zeitangabe(n) beachten!

2. a) Uncle Charles has lived/has been living in the town since 1960.

   b) He has never been to Africa up to now.

   c) Have you already seen the pyramids?/Have you seen the pyramids yet up to now?
   Hinweis: nachgestelltes *yet* nur bei Frage und Verneinung, *I haven't seen the ... yet.*

d) Have you ever visited the Benedictine Abbey in Buckfast?

e) I am so sorry. I am so tired because I've just arrived here in the abbey.

Hinweis: Die inzwischen vertraute 2. Vergangenheit, *present perfect,* zeigt nicht bloß an, dass ein Vorgang bis jetzt gilt, sondern dass er auch gerade abgeschlossen wurde.

3. a) For one year the bells have been rung by the sacristan.

b) The statue of St Christopher was stolen by gangsters.

c) Since the incident the man has been held.

d) He would be questioned all night if they had time.

e) The flat wouldn't have been moved out of/by her.

4. a) Confessing one's sins is surely troublesome.

b) But also sitting in the confessional is strenuous.

c) Listening to people's problems certainly isn't fun.

d) Walking in the abbey garden relaxes me.

e) The joyous chirping of the birds is like music in my ears.

Hinweis: Bis jetzt haben wir uns nur mit der *-ing*-Form als Objekt befasst: *I like singing* (siehe oben). Die *-ing*-Form kann aber auch Subjekt sein. Im Sinne der Lateingrammatik wird die *-ing*-Form auch als Gerund bezeichnet, besser ist die Bezeichnung *verbal noun* (gleichzeitig Zeitwort + Hauptwort!). Anstatt dieses *verbal noun* ist auch der Infinitiv zulässig: *To confess one's sins .../To sit in the confessional* usw.

f) The fathers are (just) singing the choral.

Hinweis: Verlaufsform, *progressive form*; *continuous form*, weil die Patres gerade jetzt, im Augenblick singen

g) The father said: "You are always forgetting what you promised." He said it angrily.

Hinweis: Hier haben wir eine nachdrückliche Äußerung im Sinne von Verärgerung. Aber auch bei Ungeduld oder Überraschung ist die Verlaufsform sinnvoll.

h) "I am telling it for the last time", he added.

Hinweis: Auch hier handelt es sich um eine nachdrückliche Äußerung: Verlaufsform.

i) For one hour Father Michael has been writing an essay on the Gregorian Choral

Hinweis: Die Verlaufsform drückt aus, dass er seit einer Stunde daran sitzt und noch nicht aufgehört hat, also weiterschreibt. Die Verlaufsform könnte aber auch eine Aussage anschaulicher machen. Man kann sich vorstellen, wie er da arbeitet!

j) While he was sitting in his study yesterday the bishop rang him up.

Hinweis: Das ist ein Musterbeispiel für die Verlaufsform: Ein Vorgang wird (kurz) unterbrochen. Grundsätzlich meint die Verlaufsform den Vorgang und nicht die Tatsache, dass ... Es kommt hier immer auf den Zusammenhang an. Im Übrigen wird die Verlaufsform der Gegenwart auch für die Zukunft verwendet, wenn etwas fest geplant ist: *I am travelling to the abbey tomorrow*. Vergleiche auch die anderen Zukunftsformen: *to be going* (man hat etwas vor), *will* (etwas wird geschehen, auf das man keinen Einfluss hat), schließlich die Verlaufsform der Zukunft *will be* + *-ing*: *This time next Monday I will be sitting in the confessional*: Es geschieht etwas zu einer bestimmten zukünftigen Zeit.

5. a) since

   b) since

   c) for

   d) since

   e) for

   Hinweis: Grundsätzlich mit 2. Vergangenheit; *since:* ab einem Zeitpunkt; *for:* Wie lange? Zeitraum

6. a) So do I.

   b) So did I.

   c) So have I.

   d) I won't either/Neither will I.

   e) I don't either/Neither do I.

The Car

I. Questions on the text

1. a) The hotels there have got big gardens or parks where there are enough car parks.

   b) The way between the rows of parking lots wasn't wide. The parking lots themselves weren't big.

   c) He had always maintained he was the best driver in the world.

   d) It was the first day in Italy.

   e) He thought his wife had seen the damage he had caused.

   f) His wife had damaged the car as well and he told her his mishap.

   g) She couldn't blame him as she had done the same.

   h) It was a story of an accident they had never heard of before. Everything was so silly.

   i) As everybody was laughing one workman forgot to close the left rear door.

   j) Door number 3 had been damaged before the foreman pressed the stop knob.

2. a) The couple liked the fantastic scenery there. In their view it is a very beautiful country like the Garden of Eden.

   b) In Italy there are many picturesque ancient towns with palaces and cathedrals; the climate is very mild; almost all of Italy is surrounded by seas; there are many vineyards. In Switzerland there are very high mountains, picturesque lakes, neat villages, green pastures with cattle.

   c) Car shelters protect the car from rain, the sun and from hail.

   d) They are normally smaller as the Italian streets in towns are usually narrower than anywhere else.

e) I feel some malicious joy when something happens to a person who has always said nothing can happen to him/her, or when something happens to a person that isn't just a friend of mine.

f) Number 13 just isn't a lucky number. The unlucky number 13 brings bad luck a lot of people think, and it did!

g) He might have thought about his angry wife and how she would blame him, calling him a fool.

h) I can confess my sins or faults to the parson in the confessional or to somebody else, my parents, my teachers, the friends, and to the hotel manager and the wife, of course, in our case.

i) They had to raise the platform in order to repair the car or to remove and replace the doors.

j) I can press knobs on machines, at the door, in a lift.

3. a) I must brake my car or take my foot off the accelerator.

b) I must change to a lower gear and accelerate.

c) Are the front and rear lights in order? Have I got enough fuel? Is there enough pressure in the tyres? Is the windshield clean? Where is the first-aid box?

d) Don't read the newspaper or a magazine. Don't study a map. Don't eat and drink anything. Don't kiss or hug a partner.

e) It's rather dangerous, especially for girls. You can be sexually harassed, you can be raped or even killed.

f) A car is the best shopping-bag. I can take a lot of things home which are very heavy. I am free and independent. I can go everywhere.

g) ... should be banned as it spoils the environment with the exhaust fumes, it makes a lot of noise, it causes accidents.

h) It can be reduced by more driving-lessons, by stricter laws, by drinking less alcohol, by the police carrying out checks.

i) A lot of workers are employed who pay a lot of taxes. The firms sell a lot of cars all over the world and pay purchase taxes. The workers are consumers themselves.

j) The accelerator: I can increase the speed; the brake: I brake, slow down and stop; the clutch: I need it for changing the gear(s); the steering-wheel: I steer the car.

II. Translation

1. Our couple, Mr and Mrs ..., who often go there, maintain that the Lake of Garda/Lake of Riva, which they like very much, is the most beautiful lake in their view.

   Hinweis: Wegen der englischen Satzstellung war eine Umstellung nötig. Die zwei Beifügesätze, Relativsätze, *relative clauses,* sind in beiden Fällen nicht notwendige Einschübe, deshalb Komma.

2. The hotel in which they spend their nights is less noisy than other ones.

   Hinweis: Der Beifügesatz ist wohl notwendig (welches Hotel?), deshalb kein Komma. Anstatt *which* ist auch *that* möglich, wenn Verhältniswort *in* nachgestellt. Auch: *The hotel they spend their nights in ...*

3. "Look at this wonderful/marvellous scenery/landscape", the husband always says to his wife.

   Hinweis: Verhältniswörter, Präpositionen, *prepositions,* gehen Verbindungen mit einem Zeitwort, Eigenschaftswort usw. ein; vergleiche: *to look after,* aufpassen oder *faithful to,* treu gegenüber, *laugh about,* lachen über

4. The furniture in the hotel room is also more modern than in the other hotels.

   Hinweis: Möglich auch *pieces of furniture are ...*, wenn man mehr die Einzelmöbel meint. Es gibt also Begriffe, die keine Mehrzahl bzw. keine Einzahl haben, etwa *jeans.*; siehe auch entsprechende Aufgaben in III.

5. Before they make a trip they study a lot of leaflets and maps.

   Hinweis: Diesen Zeitnebensatz, *time clause,* kann man "verkürzen". *Before making a trip ...*

6. They always have a shower after they have swum in the sea.

   Hinweis: Der Zeitnebensatz kann ebenfalls verkürzt werden: *After having swum .../After swimming .../Having swum ...*; in diesem Fall Satzumstellung vornehmen

7. As/because they like (the) Italian food, they always look forward to the supper.

   Hinweis: Auch der Grundnebensatz, Kausalsatz, *clause of reason* in anderer Form: *Liking the Italian food, they always ...*

8. As soon as they enter the dining hall they are pleased.

   Hinweis: andere Möglichkeit: *On entering the dining hall, ...*

9. They wish us to visit them once in the hotel. As we prefer to go to Norway I wish they didn't invite us.

   Hinweis: im ersten Satz die Konstruktion Zeitwort + Objekt + Infinitiv, bei einem realen Wunsch; im zweiten Satz ist der Wunsch irreal, da sie immer einladen, also *wish* + 1. Vergangenheit

10. Yesterday they telephoned and asked if we would come the following week.

    Hinweis: Der direkte Satz lautet: *"Will you come next week?"* Die indirekte Frage mit der Zeit- und Angabenverschiebung: *would, the following week*; siehe auch enstprechende Aufgaben in III.

III. Grammar

1. a) The furniture in the hotel room was modern./The pieces of furniture in the hotel room were modern.

   Hinweis: beachte: *This piece of furniture is the most modern.*

   b) On holiday she wears only elegant denim jeans.

   c) "I want to buy this pair of jeans, Miss."

   d) "A dent in the car. That is no good information/piece of information/item of information."

   Hinweis: Letztere zwei Varianten werden ganz selten verwendet.

   e) "But you have got new glasses/a new pair of glasses. That is bad news."

   Hinweis: Im Lehrbuch findest du sicher eine weitere Liste dieser Plural- und Singularbegriffe. Beim "Einzelstück" oder Einzelstücken nimmt man *piece of/pieces of* oder *item(s) of;* bei den "Dopplungen" kann man auch *pair(s) of* nehmen.

2. a) The man said (that) the car had to be repaired.

   Hinweis: andere Ersatzformen hier nicht brauchbar

   b) The man said (that) he would suggest Mayor's garage.

   Hinweis: *would* bleibt!

c) The man said by the following Wednesday Mr Mayor would have repaired his car.

d) The man said (that) if he had had the materials he would have repaired it by the following Monday.

Hinweis: Diese zwei "tiefen" Zeitstufen kann man natürlich nicht mehr verschieben.

e) The man said (that) it should be repaired indeed.

3. a) "It might have been worse."

b) "I could have had an accident."

c) "You could have been more careful."

d) "You should have been more careful, too."

e) "I must have overlooked the post."

Hinweis: Diese sogenannten Perfektkonstruktionen drücken aus, was in der Vergangenheit hätte passieren können, sollen usw.

4. a) He asked where the car was then.

b) He told me to ring Mr Mayor.

Hinweis: Beim Befehlssatz wird *say* durch *tell* ersetzt.

c) He said (that) everybody could make a mistake.

Hinweis: *was able to* passt nicht recht; es gibt übrigens auch die Regel, dass bei allgemein gültigen Aussagen keine Verschiebung stattfindet, also auch der ursprüngliche wörtliche Satz stehenbleiben könnte: *He said that everybody can make a mistake.* In der Regel kannst du dich aber darauf verlassen, dass verschoben wird, außer das berichtende Zeitwort steht in der Gegenwart usw. (siehe oben)

d) He asked by which day the car would have been repaired

e) He asked if/whether the car should be repaired at all or if it was better for him to buy a new car.

5. a) Yesterday I saw the foreman.

Hinweis: nicht verwirren lassen: Bei Zeitangabe der Vergangenheit 1. Vergangenheit, *past*

b) Have you already seen him?/Have you seen him yet?

Hinweis: "bis jetzt": 2. Vergangenheit, *present perfect*!

c) Since 1960 he worked in a hotel; then he did an apprenticeship as a mechanic; since 1975 he has worked with Mr Mayor.

Hinweis: nur wenn *since* (und *for*) an die Gegenwart heranreicht, 2. Vergangenheit, *present perfect*! *Since* (Frage 5 c Anfang) ist ohnehin ungebräuchlich, hier ist *after* korrekter

d) He promised me that the car would have been repaired by Wednesday.

Hinweis: Wörtlich sagte er: *The car will have been repaired ...* Indirekte Rede: Verschiebung zu *would have been*

e) He said that if he had had the material, he would have been able to repair it earlier.

Hinweis: Hier geht keine Verschiebung mehr. Abschließend noch zwei Beispiele, die im Zusammenhang mit der indirekten Rede den Kontrast Deutsch/Englisch zeigen: Sie sagte, sie parke. *She said she parked.* Sie sagte, sie werde parken. *She said she would park.*

6. a) We want to go to Italy again.

Hinweis: erfüllbarer, realer Wunsch!

b) But I only want you to drive.

Hinweis: erfüllbar, real!

c) But it would be nice if you would give me a second car.

Hinweis: Eigentlich müsste es heißen: *It were nice* (*if*-Satz, 2. Muster!), aber bei einer Bitte an den anderen "doppeltes" *would* möglich

d) I wish I had won in the lottery.

Hinweis: Ich wünschte ich gewänne. *I wish I won.* Das ist eher ein irrealer Wunsch, auf den man keinen Einfluss hat. Beachte, dass wünschte = *wish!*

e) If only I had won in the lottery!

List of Grammatical Terms

Latin term	German term	English term
Aktiv	Tatform	active (voice)
Passiv	Leideform	passive (voice)
	Einfache Form	simple form
	Verlaufsform	continuous form progressive form
Präsens	Gegenwart	present (tense)
Präteritum Imperfekt	1. Vergangenheit	past tense
Perfekt	2. Vergangenheit Vollendete Gegenwart	present perfect
Plusquamperfekt	3. Vergangenheit Vollendete Vergangenheit	past perfect
Futur	1. Zukunft	future
Futur Perfekt	2. Zukunft Vollendete Zukunft	future perfect
Konditional I	1. Bedingungsform	conditional
Konditional II	2. Bedingungsform	perfect conditional
(Modalverb)	Hilfszeitwort	auxiliary helping verb
Indirekte Rede	Nichtwörtliche Rede	reported speech, indirect speech
Indirekter Befehl	Nichtwörtlicher Befehl	reported imperative, indirect imperative

Indirekte Frage	Nichtwörtliche Frage	reported question, indirect question
Adverb Adverbiale	Umstandsangabe	adverb
Temporaladverbiale	Angabe der Zeit	adverb of time
	(unbestimmte Zeitangabe) Häufigkeitsangabe	adverb of frequency
Lokaladverbiale	Ortsangabe Richtungsangabe	adverb of place adverb of direction
Modaladverbiale	Art- und Weise-Angabe	adverb of manner
	Gradangabe	adverb of degree
	Steigerung, Vergleich	comparison
Infinitiv	Grundform des Verbs	infinitive
Gerund		gerund
Partizipsatz	Mittelwortsatz	participle clause
Partizip Präsens	Mittelwort der Gegenwart	present participle
Partizip Perfekt	Mittelwort der Vergangenheit	past participle
Interrogativpronomen	Fragefürwort	interrogative (pronoun)
Reflexivpronomen	rückbezügliches Fürwort	reflexive pronoun
	betonendes Fürwort	emphasizing pronoun
	wechselbezügliches Fürwort	reciprocal pronoun
Relativpronomen	bezügliches Fürwort	relative pronoun
Relativsatz	Beifügesatz	relative clause
Kausalsatz	Nebensatz des Grundes	clause of reason

Siehe auch ENGLISCH TRAINING Comprehension 9. Klasse, S. 93 f.

Ihre Meinung ist uns wichtig!

Ihre Anregungen sind uns immer willkommen.
Bitte informieren Sie uns mit diesem Schein über Ihre Verbesserungsvorschläge!

Titel-Nr.	Seite	Fehler, Vorschlag

Bitte hier abtrennen

Zutreffendes bitte ankreuzen!

Die Absenderin/der Absender ist:

- ☐ Lehrer/in
- ☐ Fachbetreuer/in
  Fächer: ____________
- ☐ Seminarlehrer/in
  Fächer: ____________
- ☐ Regierungsfachberater/in
  Fächer: ____________
- ☐ Oberstufenbetreuer/in
- ☐ Schulleiter/in
- ☐ Referendar/in, Termin 2. Staats-
  examen: ____________
- ☐ Leiter/in Lehrerbibliothek
- ☐ Leiter/in Schülerbibliothek
- ☐ Sekretariat
- ☐ Eltern
- ☐ Schüler/in, Klasse: ____________
- ☐ Sonstiges: ____________

Unterrichtsfächer: **(Bei Lehrkräften!)**

____

STARK Verlag
Postfach 1852
85318 Freising

10-V1M

Bitte ausfüllen und im frankierten Umschlag
an uns einsenden. Für Fensterkuverts geeignet.

Kennen Sie Ihre Kundennummer?
Bitte hier eintragen.

Absender **(Bitte in Druckbuchstaben!)**

Name/Vorname

Straße/Nr.

PLZ/Ort

Telefon privat
für Rückfragen

Geburtsjahr

E-Mail-Adresse

Schule/Schulstempel **(Bitte immer angeben!)**

(Bitte blättern Sie um)